SYLVIA

Tha' Don't Look Proper

by

Anne Hunt

ALD Design & Print, Sheffield

Published and Printed by:
ALD Design & Print
279 Sharrow Vale Road
Sheffield S11 8ZF
Great Britain

Telephone: 0114 268 6269

ISBN: 1-901587-02-9

First Published 1998

Inside pages printed on Risograph GR3750.

Photographs of old Sheffield by courtesy of Sheffield Newspapers.

MY LIFE, MY HOME

Where have you gone you bricks and mortar?
You that gave shelter to my mother's daughter,
And sheltered my brothers and sisters the same.
To some no more than windows and doors,
With a roof, one chimney and two floors.

Set down a hill on the side of the Don,
On a road they named after Stevenson.
You weren't a mansion, you were only small,
A living-room, a kitchen, two bedrooms, no hall.
You had no garden just a yard of stone,
With cracks round the edges where the grass had grown.

If I could go back a score years or more,
And watch my mother through the open door,
I'd see her washing and baking bread,
I'd listen a lot more to what she had said,
I'd see my brothers and sisters at play,
I'd see them in bed at the end of the day,
I'd see my father as he came in for tea,
Then fall asleep with the new on his knee.

Yes, to some no more than windows and doors,
With a roof, one chimney and two floors.
But to me, no matter where I may roam,
You were my family, my life, my home.

Anne Hunt

DEDICATIONS

To my mother:

God gave everyone a mother.
I am so thankful that you are mine.

To my dear late husband:

Thankyou for your devotion and faith in me.

CHAPTERS

CHAPTER 1

ALL PEARLS AREN'T PERFECT

It had been raining, but I had done the shopping and thankful I was too. I was heading back to the car when I saw her. She was about nine years old. She walked past me and sat on a partly demolished wall. I walked on and past her. I reached the car and, as I sat in it, I could see her. She wore a woollen cardigan and a cotton dress. The hem of the dress was reflected in a small pool of rain water.

She was so like me at her age. Her hair was a shade darker than its mid brown because of the damp weather. Her eyes were dark and round and there was a sadness about them. Her cheeks had a chubby look which gave her face a round shape, but the perfection ended there. Her top lip bore the scars of a repaired hare-lip, and her nose was a shade too big for her face, but not so much as to make her look ugly. No, she looked quite pretty in a way. As I looked at her from the car I could see she was tapping her foot in a pool of rainwater, shattering the hem of her dress in its reflection. As I sat, I felt as if I was looking back into my past, from my partly demolished wall. But my wall was as a result of the war. Hers was due to the fact that Sheffield had gone mad, building sports halls and swimming pools for the forthcoming student games. Building for the athletes of the future rather than the 'steel men' it once had.

As I sat there I think I was feeling rather sad for her, because I knew what she had already been through due to the scars on her upper lip. I couldn't help but wonder if she was going to be strong enough to take all the knocks and bangs that life had in store for her. The cruel truths of innocent children and sometimes the ignorance of adults. I wondered if she would have the courage to say to herself "I am not going to sit on a wall. I am going to go out and make people see me as a person and not as a face." I got of my wall when I was fifteen with the help of my dad, though he never knew it.

As I sat there, I hoped that she had got the kind of mother I have. One who, along with my grandmother, fought for my very life in the first few months and, through my young life, suffered very long days and sleepless nights to give me the strength and later the courage to survive. It would have been so easy for them to give in and no one would have blamed them. But I thank God and them that they held on and won.

As the rain started again the hem of her dress shattered once more in the reflection of the pool, just as my mother's pool of dreams must have been shattered that cold November morning when I, her first born, arrived.

After the delivery the midwife was shocked and tired, but she showed neither of these feelings as she said to Mum "You have a baby girl. When I have cleaned her up you can see her. Now get some rest." The nurse took me down stairs to my grandmother who was waiting for the news, boy or girl. What she didn't expect was me. The nurse told her to put me in the baby basket until the doctor had seen me. Then she remarked more to herself than to any one else "It would be a blessing if she goes." But Gran had good ears.

The nurse went back up stairs to write her notes; Sex: Girl. Date: 22 November 1937. Weight: 7 lbs 3oz. Remarks: Hare-lip with cleft palate. She closed the book. "I've left your baby downstairs so you can get some rest while I fetch the doctor." She told Gran not to disturb Mum while she had gone. Usually someone else would get the doctor but this one was up to her.

My mother woke to hear the doctor saying "what a mess." Mum, not having seen me yet, wondered what he was talking about. He looked at her and saw the expression on her face then said "Haven't you seen your baby yet mother?" and without waiting for a reply he told the nurse to give me to her. My Mum was now seeing me for the first time and her mind wasn't prepared to tell her the truth at that moment. Then she realized the doctor was saying "Yes, it is a mess, but if you are prepared to go through a lot of hard work and pain for this baby, I think something can be done for her." So the fight for my life began.

Mum put me to her breast to try to get me to suckle, but the sucking power of two lips and a roof in the mouth was just not there. She tried to express her milk straight into my mouth, but there were more misses then hits and I was in danger of being drowned or starved to death, neither of which my mother had any intention of doing. They had to have a way of getting the milk past the opening in the roof of my mouth. So my grandmother went to the chemist shop to get some advice on how to feed such an infant as I. Gran came back looking as if she had found the end to a rainbow. She produced out of her pocket a tippet, that is to say an eye dropper. It is a glass phial with a small rubber bulb at one end. This was to be my feeding bottle for the next three months. Mum had to express her milk, pick it up with the eye dropper, and get it as far back into my mouth as possible without choking me. So now I could choke to death, but Mum was insistent that I wasn't going to starve to death, a statement that was almost proved to be wrong.

At about six weeks old I was referred to the Sheffield Children's Hospital. Mum was told to bring me back in two months when I would be old enough to have my first operation. This would be the first of seventeen major and minor operations, depending on what was needed to be done.

For this first operation I was in hospital for eight weeks. Every day my mother had to express her milk, then take it up to the hospital, hand it to a nurse, turn around, and go home again. She was never allowed to see me. Visiting times were strictly adhered to then, being only once a month on a Sunday afternoon and for one hour.

At the end of my stay in hospital the nurses handed my Mother a mere skeleton of a baby. I weighed less than my birth weight. The nurses parting words to Mum were "Here Mother, do what you can for her." The doctor was right; there was going to be a lot of heartache and hard work. Mum, however, was determined that I would pull through. She went to Raymond Hall the chemist. It was the first time he had seen me. He recommended baby milk, with mother's milk in between, and Farley's rusks. Mum thought that I might be too young for these. He commented that I was too young to die as well and to try these things and see how she goes on. It was a harrowing time for her. She would take me shopping and wait for the comments; "What a lovely baby" without much conviction behind it, or "You've got your hands full love." Some even said "Wouldn't it be better to let her die love?" The 'love' came not as an endearment, but with the very outspoken

Yorkshire patter.

My father kept very much in the background in the early days. Like all fathers he wanted a perfect baby and could not accept the fact that I was not. At twenty-two the world was his oyster and the pearls that were in it had been good ones. I was the first one to have a flaw in it, so he had to have time to come to terms with it. In time he did realize that I needed two parents, not just the one, so he started to take more interest in me and what was going on. I know he loved me, but in later years he was to become more strict with me than with his six other children. He used his strictness as a shield against showing too much love and feeling in one direction. Sometimes he would get the mixture a little bit wrong. His strictness would impede on his love. Having said that he was a good father, a hard worker and he stood up for all of his family.

At the age of one year and two months I had to go into hospital again and this time my mother was heavily pregnant with her next baby. So from now on it was going to be twice as hard for her. When she took me back to the hospital the nurses could not believe that I was the skeleton baby of a year ago but, nevertheless, after my stay in hospital she was once again given back a baby skeleton. At this age some babies are walking or at least going around with the furniture. I was doing neither, because every time I went into hospital I was put into a cot and never allowed out again until I went home. So not only was I not feeding correctly, due to the fact I could only take fluids, but my muscles were not getting the exercise they needed.

My brother was born on February 13th 1939. So now my mother had two babes in arms. She has often spoken about this time of her life as being happy, despite the hardships she had to endure with me, and the threat of war looming on the horizon. At the weekends they would go on fishing trips, either for the day or for the whole weekend. Staying in a tent or with some friends who lived at the place we had gone to. It was on one of these trips that dad used his size ten boots to kick me with. Mum had put me down on the ground while she spread a blanket out for us to sit on. In a spilt second I was rolling towards my dad, who was setting up his tackle at the waters edge. My mother yelled “Look out she’s coming dad.” Dad turned to see me rolling down the slope and, without a second to think, he stuck out his foot to stop me. I think I soon learned how to walk after that.

In 1939 war was declared, but it was 1940 when my father was told to enlist for the army. However, this was not before trying an alternative, which was to go down the coal mines. He tried this and, after only one day, he had proved that he would much prefer a khaki brown suit to a pit helmet and a miners lamp. So Mum was left to fend for herself and her children and, like thousands of other women, she was pregnant again. This baby, a boy, was born late October 1940, just as Hitler chose to blitz Sheffield and the Attercliffe area in particular. We were surrounded by the steel works so we were among the enemy's prime targets. Every day we had to rush to the air-raid shelters, very often having to stay there all night if need be.

It was on such a night that I went missing. No one had seen me or knew where I had gone. My mother was going mad, ordering the home-wardens not to just stand there but to go and look for me. She must have been out of her mind with worry. Not me! I had gone walkabout and was watching the bright lights of the exploding bombs. I was, however, found and put into the nearest shelter. The news was given to my mother that I was safe, but due to the heavy bombing, I had to stay where I was. I never got out to see the bright lights again. It wasn't all doom and gloom. There were pockets of humour as well.

The morning after a bombing raid my Mum saw a woman scooping water out of a horse trough. Mum commented that it wouldn't be fit to drink. "Never mind that," said the woman "my old feller needs a drink when he gets home and this'll do." Little did Mum realize that she would be drinking the same water a couple of days later. We were all down in the shelter again and Mum was breast feeding the baby. She remarked how breast feeding always made her feel thirsty and that she would love a cup of tea. Hearing that, my aunty who was staying with us at the time, said "Don't worry Annie. I'll go and get some water to mash with." If she had been seen leaving the shelter she would have been in real trouble or, even worse, she could have been killed. She went into some of the houses to get water from the tap but they were all dry, so she went to the trough. She divided the soot and dirt that laid like a lid on top of the water and, through the gap, she scooped a pan full of the precious liquid. She took it back to the shelter where she boiled it and mashed a pot of tea. Mum drank it then said that it was one of the best cups of tea she had had in a long time. It was a long time afterwards when she found out where the water had come from for it.

A couple of nights later, one of Hitler's bombs had our address on it. As we came out of the shelter people saw the devastation. It was a lot worse then anyone had imagined. Our house, though it had been hit, was not as bad as some. It was not safe to live in. Most of the windows were gone and half of the roof was blown off. At least we still had a front door, until Mum tried to open it then it fell off. Everybody just fell about laughing. Laughing released a lot of the tension in those days.

The next day Mum gathered together what few things she could carry. She loaded them on to the baby's pram, laid baby Kenneth on the top of our hastily packed belongings and started to walk the six miles to Shirecliffe, where my great grandmother lived. However, within a few days we were on the road again due to a quarrelsome aunt who would not leave us or Mum alone. We were on the road but this time Mum didn't know where we were going or where we would be sleeping that night, as we walked towards Sheffield city centre. We could not go to Gran's because her home had been bombed too, so Mum just walked. It was quite by chance that we met an old friend of hers. We came to know her as Aunty Hilda and she was our miracle. She saw the state my mother was in and, without hesitating, took us back to her home. It was only small and there were four people already living there, but that didn't matter. They all moved over, chipped in and made us very welcome. I can't say how long we stayed there, but that was the spirit of the war. People like Aunty Hilda, small miracles, pockets of humour, and plenty of guts like my mother had. However, the happiness she found there was short lived. The long walks in the icy winds were to take their toll. My father was home on leave to try and repair the damage to our house, but instead he had to help nurse his dying son, Kenneth. He was just six weeks old when he died on Christmas eve 1940.

In 1942 the war was still raging and I was to go into hospital for yet another operation. This one was to try and close the gap in my top lip. It was my fifth, but it was one of the first I can remember. I can't recall much, only the sister that came and told me off. I had come round from the anaesthetic and was conscious enough to take note of what was going on around me. I laid watching a nurse with a tray. She was going from bed to bed giving fruit or sweets to the patients. She served someone in the next bed to mine then she turned and smiled at me. I must have looked like a broken doll laying there, because she came to me and as she put a sweet on the table she said "I'll leave that there, and when you are better you can have it." Then she was gone. As soon as she had disappeared the sister came into the ward. She saw the sweet and with that 'I'm in charge' look on her face she said "You naughty girl. I told you not to eat anything until you are told. You know you shouldn't have these don't you?" Then she and my sweet had gone. It was the first time I had been misjudged and it hurt deeply. The operation was not a success either. The cleft in the lip was too wide and needed a skin graft.

By the time I started school I had gained a sister. I remember my first day at school. As Mum was getting me ready she kept saying "Don't worry you'll be all right love." Now she never said this when I was going into hospital. I suppose, like me, she had got used to me going there, but this was different. I remember walking into the class room and feeling very scared. The hand that took me away from my mother wasn't as gentle as the nurses in the hospital. I had learned to accept the ward and all that went with it, but this was definitely different.

I was a little older than the other children in the class due to my stay in hospital. I started well into the new term, in the baby class. The Wendy-House was to be my second home and I resented anyone else who tried to get in with me. A few weeks later I was moved to another class, more my own age group. There was no Wendy-House here. Where ever I went there was always someone looking at me. It was usually the older children and I always knew I was in for a rough ride when there was a gang of them. I soon learned the art of latching on to other groups who were more friendly. I have had a few heroes in my life who would come to my rescue when things were getting a bit out of hand, but that didn't mean I couldn't stick up for myself if needs be.

I was almost seven years old when the buff coloured envelope dropped through the door. I was beginning to have mixed feelings about this going into hospital business. On the one hand it was good, because I wouldn't have to go to school for a long time. I would get some new knickers and vests and sometimes, if Mum had the money and the clothing coupons left, I would get a new dress. The latter didn't happen very often. The actual fact of being in the hospital didn't worry me either and the operation, though not welcomed, I took in my stride. It was the fact that I wouldn't see my brothers and sisters for a long time, sometimes up to six weeks. The visiting times were so far apart and only two to a bed for half an hour and no changeover. It was hard to remember peoples faces. I would get scared when I couldn't remember Mum or Gran's faces. Dad's face was just a photograph on the sideboard due to him being in the army. It's funny, but I could always remember that. There was the added worry of the ward sister this time; Would she still think it was me who asked for that sweet and would she still be mad at me? When Mum and I arrived at the hospital we went into the now familiar big ward and, for the first time, Mum was allowed to undress me and put me into bed. She still wasn't allowed to stay any length of time. The visiting times were still strictly adhered to, but they were a bit more often now. They were Wednesday evenings, Saturday afternoons and evenings, and Sunday afternoons. However, they were still only for the half hour each visit and no changing over.

I was used to the hospital routine, but couldn't help feeling like I was a little boat in a big sea. The ward seemed to go on for ever and the beds were countless. There was always someone crying somewhere. I was used to it so it didn't worry me, but it must have been frightening for the older children who were in for the first time. The nurses were like my friends. When they came on duty they would come to my bed saying "Hello Nancy. Have you come back to see us?" and very often they would give me a hug. I was waiting to see the sister come through the doors but I had to wait until the following day. I had to get through the night with the thought going around in my head. In the morning, before breakfast, the doors of the ward opened and there she was coming down the ward and heading straight for my bed, "Hello Nancy. How are you today? It's nice to see you again." I was relieved that she hadn't remembered, like I had, and I was only six! Six or not I was to learn what fear and pain were really like.

I was to be in hospital for quite a while this time before the operation. In the past I was in one or two days at the most before going down to theatre, but this time it was different. I was having tests and x-rays, my mouth was being measured and every time I asked "why?" I was told "Don't worry. You'll be all right." Now, from past experience of being told not to worry, I was beginning to be very scared. A few days passed by without anything happening at all and I was beginning to think that they might have forgotten about me. I wasn't worried. I felt a kind of safeness while I was in here. In hospital I hadn't got to face up to reality that I was slightly different from the others. So, instead of

Mother, father, brother Archie and myself aged 4

Left to right, myself, sister Ivy, Mum and brother Archie, 1943

A typical Sheffield East End row of terraced houses

My first school photograph, 4th July 1944, aged seven

becoming more worried, I was becoming more contented. However, my contentment came to an abrupt end one morning when, without any warning, the now familiar preparations were started.

I was given an enema and bathed. Then I was wrapped in a big white sheet or towel and put back into bed. The thing I never did like and still don't like is having the screens put around the bed. I always wanted to say "Don't do that", but I wouldn't have dared. So the screens were coming down the ward towards me with their familiar noise. It sounded like a lot of chattering little mice. They would stop as they got to my bed, then chatter some more as the nurse put the screen in place. Then she and the mice were gone.

I looked up at the ceiling. I could just see two of the goldfish bowl lamp shades, with the thin layer of gray dust around the top half giving way to the white colour underneath. It looked as if the lights were wearing little mop caps. I let my mind wonder to more sinister thoughts. I wondered if this is what dying was like. After all, it had happened twice while I was in this time. The nurses had told everybody who could walk about to stay in bed, then they put screens around a bed. They would be there for a long time. When the screens were moved there was nobody there, not even the bedding. It was due to an epidemic I was told. "What's an epidemic?" I asked, but I was never told the answer.

To get away from my thoughts I started to look around. The curtains had little flowers on them and one or two tiny holes. Through these I could see the sun flicking its light on and off. I saw the note that was stuck to my bed with sticking plaster 'nil by mouth.' It was the first time I had been able to read this notice.

I heard footsteps coming down the ward and I knew that they were coming towards me. The screens opened and the nurse said "Hello Nancy. You know what this is don't you?" She had the kidney shaped dish in her hand. The needle went into my leg and out again, leaving the now familiar stinging pain. This injection would make me very thirsty and, at the same time, a very tired feeling would come over me making it very difficult for me to summon enough energy to ask for a drink of water, for which I was desperate. At last the nurse did come round the screens to look at me and ask if I was all right. I shook my head and asked for a drink. All she would say was "Try to sleep. It will all be over soon." Then she was gone, leaving me to fight the inevitable sleep.

I was regaining consciousness after the operation on my top lip. I shall always remember the feeling of extreme fear as I woke up and felt my hands had been bandaged. I was convinced that I had had my hands cut off until a voice spoke to me through the haze of sleep and anaesthetic, reassuring me that my hands had not been cut off, but were only bandaged to stop me pulling at the large plasters that covered my cheeks. I had a brace on my top lip and the plasters were there to keep the brace in place. I don't know to this day why I had the brace on, or what purpose it served. I only know the day that they took it off will live with me for ever.

I heard the mouse sounds of the screens coming down the ward. I would be relieved when they passed my bed or stopped before they got to me, but today they didn't stop or go past. The nurse danced the screens into position around my bed and told me that I was having my brace off today. Then she was gone. It had been a month since I thought my hands had been cut off. I was allowed to leave the bandages off for a week after the operation.

I was in the midst of my thoughts when two nurses came around the screens with a trolley. They put a waterproof bib under my chin and tied it at the back of my neck. Then they proceeded to bathe around my mouth and top lip. The solution stung into the sore areas and quite a bit ran into my mouth. It was very foul tasting stuff. The nurses did their best not to hurt me too much. This done, one of the nurses disappeared. When she returned she was wearing a mask. I could tell she was smiling by the way her eyes closed a little and little lines appeared at the sides of them. I was still looking at her when two unknown masked doctors came round the screens and they said the two words I did not want to hear, "Don't worry." My alarm bells began to ring. One of the doctors told my smiling nurse to hold my arms and the other nurse to hold my head still. In this position I saw the nurse in front of me turn her face away and, just as she did, a resounding pain, such as I have never known before or since, covered me around my ears, and down my neck, and then again down the other side. They continued to remove the brace then one doctor said to the other "This girl is allergic to plaster." The tears were streaming down either side of my face as my smiling nurse took me in her arms and held me. It was a long time before my cheeks stopped hurting and itching and I was allowed to go home.

Home for me was a two up, two down, small terraced house in a row of nine houses and one shop, in a street surrounded by houses on three sides and a large steel making firm on the other. That was until the war came and Hitler decided to rearrange the street by blowing up the houses opposite. The powers that be didn't rebuild the houses, but put up a big steel firm instead. So now we had steel firms on two sides of us.

As I walked down the street every house had white steps and some had whitened their window sills. All the houses had net curtains. These were always white and it seemed that there was a competition for who's were the whitest. The fronts of the houses were swept every Friday, usually late afternoon when the steel works were shutting down for the weekend. Then we would swill the paving stones with the water we had used to wash the house steps with. It was a kind of indication that the weekend had come.

Attercliffe Council School on Stevenson Road was just a few yards away from where I lived. It was one of the bigger schools in Sheffield before it was bombed in the war. Now it made an excellent playground for the children of the area. To sit at a desk in a classroom with no roof on and no teacher in it was a child's dream. Hitler gave us lots of these playgrounds; offices, shops, works or houses. The bigger buildings were the more exciting to play in and the imagination could, and would, run riot and so did the kids on the streets.

On warm summer nights the children and the men would sit out on the wide window sills, while the women would bring out the high backed chairs, always well polished. I remember an old lady, Mrs. Taylor. She was always carried out by the men. She would be still sitting in her chair then, when she was ready, they would carry her back in again. The men would be talking amongst themselves, but as soon as any young people got near they were told, in no uncertain manner, to go and play near their mothers. What could be so secret that we weren't allowed to listen to was beyond me. Try as I might to stay in earshot, they would not continue until we had gone.

The women folk would be crocheting, sewing or knitting and it would always baffle me how they could knit so quickly and talk at the same time never dropping a stitch. This little scene was acted out with jugs of ale for the men, fetched earlier by the wives, or children. The latter would make sure they'd had a taste of it behind a corner before handing it over to the men. There would be pots of tea for the women, usually in half pint mugs. Some of the ladies wouldn't say no to a drop of the men's beer, and something a little bit stronger in their tea.

Inside, the houses were small and compact. Our house was the entry house, but we didn't have the bit that went over the entry. So our bedrooms were very small and very crowded, with six children eventually to be living there. We had a living room and a kitchen. The kitchen was dominated by a large pot sink. At the side of this was a wash copper. This copper would be turned into a bath when the washing had been done. Mum would have to put a towel on the bottom to stop our feet burning because the fire that had been used to heat it up would still be smouldering underneath. At the side of the copper was a mangle. On wash days this would be dragged out into the yard and used to squeeze all the excess water out of the clothes before they were hung out on the lines to dry. Then later it would become a press for the sheets before they were aired and very often put back on the bed the same day. The curtains would get the same treatment but it wouldn't matter if they weren't quite dry. They would have to be hung up the same day before it went dark, being the only pair Mum had. We had no cooker, just two gas rings that my father had fixed up. The oven cooking was done in the fire oven in the front room. I can still smell the cooking of bread and some of the best Yorkshire puddings I have ever tasted came out of that oven. The fireplace was black leaded every Saturday morning before breakfast and, before the fire was lit, you would consider yourself very lucky if it went first time. A big cast iron kettle would be filled with water and this would sit on the fire for most of the day, giving us the luxury of hot water when needed. Needless to say we had to wash in cold water every morning.

In the living-room opposite the fire stood the sideboard, my mother's pride. It was polished every week without fail and later this job was given to me. She would know if I had just skimmed over it. In front of this was a large wooden table. There was no polish left on this, so it was always covered with a flower patterned oil cloth that we could wipe clean if anything was spilt on it. There was little room left between the fire and the table, but it would have been unthinkable to get rid of such a good strong table like that. So after every meal it would be pushed back against the sideboard, but never quite touching it.

As the family got bigger, the space got less and less. We had three arm chairs. One was my father's, and you risked life and limb if you sat in it when he was there. Even visitors got a look that said "move" and though he was away in the army, it still felt like an achievement to sit in it without him knowing.

Mum was a proud woman and kept a clean house although the odds were very much against her, with the muck and soot from the works around us. She had to substitute a lot of things because of the rationing and shortage of cash and goods in the shops. She would use salt in the water instead of disinfectant. We always bought bath size soap when we could get it. This would be cut in half and we never threw the ends away either. These would be made into soft soap and used in the soaking bucket for the babies' nappies.

Syrup or treacle would be substitute for sugar in a lot of weird and wonderful ways, as was a newspaper. This would make a good draught stopper. It would make a very good table cloth when the only one we owned was in the wash, or was being saved for someone who was coming to have a meal with us. I have sat for hours cutting it into six inch square pieces, then threading string through one corner. This bunch of papers would then be put in the toilet to be used as and when needed, but not before you had read the bits of news. It would be very frustrating to be reading something and it would end mid sentence. We read the paper more in there than we ever did in the house. The towels would end their days as guest towels or flannels. A coat would make patchwork blankets, or end up as a pegged rug, but only if it was no use for the next one down.

Sheets had the longest life. Mum always bought double sized. Again it was cheaper this way. The old double sheets would be cut in half to make single sheets, or cot sized sheets. These in turn would become pillow cases, or handkerchiefs for little noses. The list is endless but, despite the poverty, no one looked down on you because every one was in the same boat. When the real hard times came, you were never more than a door away from help and friendship.

The time came for me to go back to school, after my long stay in hospital and time at home to recuperate. 'Recuperate' was another way of saying 'staying at home for as long as possible and using every excuse in the book to do just that.' But now the time was here and I was just as nervous as if it was my first day at school. As we got to the infants gate, Mum said “We’re not going in there today love. You are going to the big school.” So, we went into the juniors gate, across the yard and up the stone steps into Huntsman’s Gardens School. Not the most appropriate name for there wasn’t a garden in sight. We knocked on the head masters door. After the formalities of being enrolled into the new school, my mother went home and I was taken to my new class.

I was shown into the first class in the juniors. In an instant I could see that they were all older than me. So now, instead of being the oldest in class, I was the youngest. I would have started the junior school after Christmas, but there was only a few weeks to go so, instead of getting me settled back into the infants only to be moved again, someone thought it best if I moved now. No-one asked my mother, or me what we thought about it. So here I was, prematurely in the big school, not knowing anyone or anything and feeling more nervous than ever.

All the class rooms lead out into a large circular hall. It had the appearance of being a sunken arena. The three steps doubled as seats and they went all the way round, except at one side, where the Heads office was. In front of his door the steps gave way to smaller steps. You were never allowed to short cut across the hall. To do so was a punishable offence so, when you were called in from playtime or you were late, it was very tempting to cross it, especially when the door you needed was bang opposite. The girls and boys were separated into their own yards and the doors were on opposite sides to each other. Everyone had to walk around the hall in a clockwise direction.

In class I was put in the front row. I didn’t contribute much to any of the lessons. It just seemed like I sat there and listened. I understood very little of what was going on around me. I only felt useful when there was an errand to be done or papers to be collected or given out. When my peers from the infants joined the class everything changed. I would be expected to know as much as them, if not a little bit more than them now.

After Christmas I was much happier. Having my peer group around me again my confidence grew and I started to answer questions verbally. Inevitably the teacher would say “Pardon” or “Would you repeat that please Nancy?” I know, because of my cleft palate, it was hard for her to understand what I was saying, but it did get a little bit monotonous to have to repeat everything I said. So I was faced with a decision;

When the teacher wanted a verbal answer should I risk not being understood and thus give the others a chance to make fun of me afterwards, or should I keep quiet even if I did know the answers. I chose the latter of the two, so now when the teacher asked I just didn't put my hand up and this decision made the teachers think that I had lost interest or that I didn't try to answer. They thought perhaps I was going deaf so I was given a hearing test which, needless to say, was negative. I was told to pull myself together and stop being lazy.

As time passed by I noticed that I was being put further and further to the back of the class. I tried to tell myself it was because I was a bit taller than the others, or maybe I was a bit cleverer than the rest. After all I had been in the class a bit longer than most of them. Then one day I had a cruel argument with a 'best friend.' I don't remember the cause, but it must have been very important to two seven year olds. Nevertheless, her parting words were the most cruel I would ever hear. She went away shouting "Don't think it's because you're clever that you're sat at the back of the class. It's because no-one wants to see you." It was like being told there was no Father Christmas. My confidence went down to zero. I went home and looked in the mirror saying to my mother "Am I ugly Mum?" My Mum, bless her, said "No you're not" and just pooh-poohed it as if I was asking the time. She said no more but went out to the neighbours next door. In next to no time our neighbour came in so I said "Mum has just gone to your house Kerkhoff." 'Kerkhoff' was the family name and we used it very affectionately without the Mr. or Mrs. "It's all right love. She's staying in our house for a little while. She's not feeling very well." Oh, the innocence of children!. After this I was to develop an inferiority complex which was a mile high and lasted until I was fifteen years old. Then things changed, including my name, but while I was at this school I would be first out at playtimes just so I could disappear to the solitude of the toilets, or a part of the playground where I hoped no-one would notice me until the bell rang to return to the class. The sharp edge of my friend's words did soften after a time, but I was never to forget them.

After my last traumatic stay in hospital I was terrified of going back there, even though it was only for check-ups. Mum often said that she never understood the change in me after I had come out of hospital and gone back to school. I became moody and withdrawn. I suppose, as a child, I didn't want to admit that I had been hurt, both mentally and physically. Besides, you don't cry where I come from. Not even the girls, or at least not in public.

A few weeks after starting the 'big' school I had a letter saying that I should attend the Sheffield Royal Hospital outpatients department at the said date and time. Now, this was a new hospital to me and I was disappointed at its appearance when we arrived there. It was an old black building in the middle of Sheffield. At the same time a little of my fear had gone because this was a new hospital and nothing about it related to my past experiences. So a little of my confidence returned with this new adventure.

My mother and I were told to go to the end of a corridor and sit in the waiting room. I swear that corridor was a mile long and it was so cold as we sat in the waiting room. I had never seen a ceiling that was so high. The walls were tiled from floor to ceiling. The bottom half was green and the top half was white. The white had gone a dirty cream colour with a film of dirt over all. Most of the tiles were crazed and the only clean parts were around light switches or where people had leaned on the walls while waiting for a seat. We sat on a wooden bench and, after what seemed like a lifetime, my name was called and we were taken into another room. This room was tiled again, but a bit cleaner. In it was a large black chair. The nurse lifted me up and sat me in it. She put a big white cape in front of me. Just as she was doing this a man came in and started talking to Mum. After a few minutes he came over to me. He took my little hand in his and said "Don't look so scared Nancy. I'm not going to bite you. You will probably bite me first." I liked him. He went on to tell me that I was going to have some false teeth. Now at seven years old I had never heard of false teeth, let alone seen them. So now my mind ran riot. How were they going to stay in my mouth? How was I going to eat my food with all those extra teeth in it? What if I swallowed them? Would I get in to trouble? The self questioning and doubt was endless. I had made up my mind I wasn't going to like these new teeth one little bit. I can't recall the dentists name so I will call him 'Mr. Mann.' The nurse gave him a mask and then came the familiar command "Open wide please Nancy." After the initial inspection was made with the dentist pulling my mouth one way then the other and talking to Mum in between, it was decided that I should come back next week. So an appointment was made. I remember

Huntsman's Gardens School, shown here in 1979

The Royal Hospital on West Street, replaced by The Hallamshire in 1978 and demolished in the early 1980's

Mum always gave me some sweets on the way home.

The following week we arrived at the hospital. As we walked up the long corridor I still could not understand why I couldn't have any breakfast. Maybe we hadn't got time. Mum was always rushing when we had to go somewhere. We sat in the cold tiled waiting room. It wasn't long before my nurse came out to us. She took my hand, but I didn't see the small gesture telling Mum to stay where she was. As I was led away to the 'chair room' Mr. Mann said "Hello Nancy." At this moment I realized Mum wasn't with me. He must have noticed the panic in my face because he picked me up and as he sat me in the chair he was saying "Don't worry" and, for once, I didn't. The nurse started to ask me lots of questions; Had I had anything to eat or drink that morning? Did I go to the toilet before I came? Did I want to go now? I didn't talk I just shook or nodded my head as an answer. It was about now I was desperately wanting to go to my Mum, but then Mr. Mann came back. He had put his hat on and he looked a bit funny. He bent down to me and cupped my chin in his hand and said "Now Nancy, I'm just going to send you to sleep for a short while and when you wake up your Mummy will be here with you." I was to be one of the youngest people to have dentures. The substance that was used then was very slow to set. They knew that it would have been a problem for a seven year old to keep still and not to panic when the substance started to harden. So to make a good impression of my mouth it was necessary to put me to sleep. When it was all over it was up to Mum to get me home. We couldn't afford a taxi so Mum had to virtually carry me home. I must have been one big dead-weight to carry that day. My only recollections of the rest of that day was a foul smell in my nose and a taste of a chalky substance in my mouth that made me feel very thirsty.

A couple of days later Mum received a letter telling her that I would have to have the whole thing done again. I was to find out later that, rare as it was to make false teeth for a seven year old, to make some for an infant with a cleft palate was unheard of to say the least. So Mr. Mann, my Mum and myself were all on an unknown road. The appointed day arrived and this time Mum did say "Don't have anything to eat or drink this morning love." I remembered thinking my Mum lied to me because, going back home on the tram last week, she had told me that I wouldn't have to go through that again, well not for a long time any way. I can not recall the journey to the hospital that day, only the time when it came to go into the chair room. The door to the waiting room opened. She was a stranger this nurse and the fears of old came rushing back into my body. My mothers heart must have been torn to pieces as I was led away crying with the nurse hanging on to my very stretched arm. Even the very nicely spoken Mr. Mann could not console me this time. So I sat there in the big chair with tears streaming down my face. Then, without warning, the face mask came from behind on to my face and just as I was going to try and pull it off Mr. Mann held my arms and said "It's all right. You've had it done before." and as last week he tried to get me to count the drops from the bottle that was dripping liquid on to the mask, but this week I didn't start to count. The rest of the day was spent in a daze.

It must have been the most nailbiting time of my mother's life, worrying if (a) she had made the right decision for me. After all it may not have worked out then I would have gone through all this for nothing, and (b) if the making of the teeth were a success, would I be able to cope with them? I went to school the next day telling everyone I was going to get some new teeth. I was very careful not to say false teeth. I'd convinced them into thinking I was going to grow them. I'd said it so often I almost believed it myself.

On the next visit to hospital I was much calmer and it was my nurse who came through the door. 'He' picked me up and said "That's better. Let me see you smile." Then he sat me in the chair and the nurse put a little white cape over me. The dentist had disappeared. When he came back into the room he was holding what appeared to be a big ball of chalk. He put it on the table and turned away to put his face mask on. I looked at the chalk. It was in two halves. I could just see a little bit of pink colour. He lifted the top half of the chalk, now I could see the rest of the pink. He said "These are going to be your new teeth Nancy, but there is a lot more work to be done on them." He took the small pink palate out. The size of his thumb nearly stopped me from seeing anything at all until he held it by the edges. I didn't like it. It had no white teeth and it looked too big for me. It was as if he had read my mind when he said "Don't worry. We're going to put you some nice little teeth at the front and they will look just like real ones. Open." He put the palate into my mouth and immediately I started retching. He soon whipped them out again saying "I'll take some off the back then they won't touch your throat." He went into the next room. While the nurse was talking to me I could hear a scraping and grinding noise coming from the room. Mr. Mann came back drying the palate on a piece of gauze. He put the palate back into my mouth and this time it was better, though I waited for the reaction. He looked at me from every angle; from the sides, from the front, he went to the back of me and looked down from the top of my head, which I thought was very odd at the time. I have since learned that it was to see if the front protrusion he had put on the teeth was too much.

He looked at me and asked if they felt all right. I nodded my head, but he said "I can't hear you." "Yes" I replied. I had said my first word with a palate covering the hole in the roof of my mouth and it didn't sound like me at all. Mr. Mann and the nurse were both smiling and looking at me. It seemed a long time since I had seen Mum, but as we went home I told her about the new teeth I was going to get.

Our next appointment was a week later. The palate had got the promised teeth in front. Mr. Mann put them in for me saying "Smile. That's wonderful. Let's have Mum in." The nurse went out, and came back with her. I had been told what to say: "Hello Mum. Do you like my new teeth?" and then the instructed smile. I could see I had made her cry.

We had two more consecutive visits then the penultimate one. For weeks before this visit I was being told by my Mum and Grandma that soon I would be speaking a lot better and when I smile, I will have some lovely white teeth to show. Whereas now there was just a gap. I had come to the conclusion Mum was trying to convince herself more than me that everything would be all right. The day for the hospital arrived and, for once, we were early and didn't have to hurry up the long corridor. We sat in the waiting room and for the hundredth time Mum was saying "Now you will try to keep them in won't you?" Just then the nurse appeared. She doesn't have to call my name these days. I just hold her hand and we go in together. I looked back at Mum. She was just sitting there looking down into her lap with her fingers interlaced with each other.

When I was sat in the chair with my white bib on, Mr. Mann asked me if some of his friends could have a look at me with my new teeth in and, if I said yes, he might let me go home with the teeth today. I think I would have agreed to anything that day. With his nod, the nurse opened the door and all the people came in; some in white coats, some in black ones, but all of them looking at me. My nurse came back from the door and held my hand. Mr. Mann was talking to all the people in the room. He was explaining that I was born with a double hare-lip and cleft palate; that there was very little bone structure for the nose, hence the flatness of the nose and virtually no throat structure; that there was no gum at the front of the mouth. He gave it a fancy name, but I knew what he meant; also that I had no way of growing my own teeth in the top front area of the mouth, but that I had done remarkably well with what I had and I was managing to keep this palate in my mouth. Then he said to me "So lets try it Nancy." He turned around to face me and, as he was putting in the teeth, he winked and said "Here we go." He stepped aside from me, then he asked me to say the nursery rhyme 'Mary Mary quite contrary.' We had been doing this rhyme from the first time he put the toothless pink palate into my mouth, so the request didn't come as a surprise. However, the applause was and everyone was saying "well done." At this point I saw Mr. Mann talking to the nurse, who then went out of the room. She came back with my mother. Mr. Mann told me to say the nursery rhyme for her. When I had done I could not understand why she was crying and all the other people were happy.

I would describe this time of our lives as our mountain, Mr. Mann's and mine, but most of all Mum's. On the way home on the tram nothing had changed. Mum asked me if I would like to go to Gran's to show her my new teeth. I nodded in agreement then she asked me if I wanted a sweet and, of course, I said "Yes please". It was a toffee. It began to get softer and softer and very, very gooey. Anyone who wears dentures knows that toffees are not friends with dentures and there was a big fight going on in my mouth. Well, by now I was thinking; do I swallow the sweet and hope that my teeth don't go down with it, or do I show Mum? I chose the latter, so with no more ado I took the teeth out with the toffee well attached to them and gave them to her saying "They are stuck." I can't remember anyone's reaction to this little scene, but Mum can and often reminds me of it. She had obviously not thought of the consequences of toffee verses teeth. We arrived at my grandmother's in floods of laughter and there was more to come. Gran asked me if I could show her my new teeth so I promptly took them out to show her. In a fit of panic Mum said "I don't think your grandma meant for you to take them out love. In future if any one asks to see them just smile love, that's all."

At first, eating with the teeth in was very difficult so I was allowed to eat without them for a time, but then I started to find I was halfway through a meal before I realized I'd still got them in. In the early days my mouth was quite often very sore and, as I have said before, you don't cry down our street. So I developed a very high pain barrier. As time went on I did get used to them, but it still felt as if I was speaking with my mouth full, so at night under the cover of darkness and bed blankets, I would take the teeth out and listen to my self talking. The difference was, and still is, amazing. So after a time they became second nature to me.

I went back to school and for the first time I was made to feel different by the teachers instead of the pupils. Now the teachers became very protective towards me, or was it my teeth? Because I wouldn't take the teeth out I wasn't allowed to go swimming, I wasn't allowed any ball games for fear of being hit in the mouth and physical training periods were limited to standing exercises only. At such times as these I would have to go to some other class, or told just to watch. To watch was more frustrating than being sent to another class. So to vent my frustrations I used to trampoline on the bed, or I would go out with friends, both boys and girls, to a place were no adult would dare to go. There we would swing on ropes or climb trees then dare each other to jump, each time from a higher branch. Here, there would be no adult or teacher telling me what I could and couldn't do. In school at this time it was one long battle against teachers being over protective and my peers chastising me whenever they got the chance.

CHAPTER 2

NO FATHER CHRISTMAS

Nine days after my seventh birthday my brother Keith was born. He was Mum's fourth child and born on December 1st 1944. My father was still in the army and the world was still at war. So now Mum needed me at home to look after her and our new baby. The school inspector, known better as the school 'Bobby', was always at our house, but instead of telling Mum off for keeping me off school, I would make him a cup of tea and he and Mum would pass the time of day, while I held the baby and kept on eye on my sister Ivy. My brother Archie would be at school. New Mums weren't allowed out of bed for ten days after giving birth. The midwife would come around any time of the day to try and catch you out of bed and if she did it was as if you had committed murder. So on no account was Mum getting out of bed. When I did get back to school I would have to hurry home and call for my sister from the neighbours who would often say "I'll keep her while you've had your teas." Then I would put into the oven whatever Gran had left for us. It might be some stew or broth or a meat and potato pie. I don't remember this time as being hard work. I was in charge of my family and that felt good. I was the little mother. When Gran was not around I would get my brother and sister into bed then leave Mum some hot water in the kettle. The tea making things were kept in a small cupboard by the bed and the bottle of milk was stood in cold water. Then it was time for me to go to bed, but not before our last cup of tea together. That's when Mum would tell me about the letters from Dad and any other news she thought I might be interested in. Next morning the whole thing would start again, getting my brother and sister ready and sat down for breakfast. At which time Gran or a neighbour would be in to see to Mum and the baby and get me and my brother off to school. We learned at a very early age to be independent of grown ups.

Before the baby was born, dad had written to Mum promising her that he would never leave England until she had had the baby. A promise Mum thought futile because if 'they' wanted him to go overseas 'they' wouldn't ask him if he wanted to go, not likely! So Mum laid no score against that promise.

They both had secret ways of sending messages to each other. One was a black map. Dad had a black map and if he sent it home it meant that he was leaving the country. When he returned he would take the map back with him. A few days before the baby was born the map had come. Mum was crying for most of the day and kept saying "Why?" Our baby was two days old when my father decided to pay us a visit. I was in the kitchen washing up the pots before getting my brother and sister to bed, when all of a sudden the back door flew open and a man dashed in. For a few moments there was sheer panic. Mum was shouting from her bed in the front room "Who is it Nancy?" and "Come in here" all in one breath. It took a second to recognize my father. He put his finger to his lips and said "sh" and then he went in to the living room. I heard Mum say "Archie! What are you doing here?" I thought the last question was a bit daft because he lived here, so I didn't understand why she had asked him that. Other things that puzzled me at the time were why he looked like he did; His face was dirty and unshaven, his usually very smart uniform was dirty and he wasn't wearing his hat. He had told me once that his hat was the most important part of his uniform because it had the badge on it. Also, why didn't he want us to tell any one? Our dad was home!

I wasn't old enough then to realize the enormity of the situation and the position he had got himself into. He had always promised Mum that he would get home to see that everything was all right with her and the baby. I was to learn later that he kept his promise to Mum against massive odds. He must have been very frustrated when he was on the docks in Scotland, waiting for a ship to take him to who knows where and his promise to Mum going around and around in his head. He had been told that the baby was born and everything was all right, but he couldn't be certain that this hadn't been said just to get him onto the boat peaceably. He always had me at the back of his mind whenever the children were born. In fact, he didn't believe the authorities at all. So now here he was trying to make his mind up; The slings and arrows of cupid or the guns and bullets of war. His mind was made up for him when fate took a hand. He was passing the trains that brought the soldiers to the docks when he saw the name 'Sheffield' on a display board at the end of one of the platforms. However, there were two trains, one on either side of the platform. So which was it? Because of the war the actual destination of any train was never carried on display. If you were in doubt you had to ask a guard or a porter, but dad was going to be no ordinary traveller. He could not ask anyone and he had made up his mind. He was going home. I never did get to know the full facts about that journey, but he must have loved Mum very dearly to do that for her and his new son, Keith Malcolm Mallender.

The next morning my brother, sister and I were allowed to stay at home. We were sat down having dinner when there was a loud knock at the door and two military policemen came in. Seeing them was so frightening, but my father, being who he was, asked them if they wanted a cup of tea while he ate his dinner. When dad had gone Mum said that they had taken him to the 'glass house, a term used for the imprisonment of military personnel. The term 'glass house' is derived from the barracks at Aldershot where they had a glass roof, not as the one at Somm Barracks in Sheffield. We didn't know when, or even if, we would see our dad again. Desertion was a capital offence in war time and it carried very heavy reprimands for any soldier who dared to do it. Whatever dad did or said worked, because within a few days he was back home with compassionate leave to boot. He had the luck of the devil and the blarney of the Irish, so Mum would say. He'd promise the earth if it got him what he wanted. However, not quite this time because I know that if he could have stayed with us for Christmas he would have done.

I was to find out there was no Father Christmas this year. Mum was still sleeping downstairs so that she could keep the fire going and keep the baby warm. Losing her baby through pneumonia as she did must have made her very wary of the cold nights. It was lovely for us older children to get up on a cold frosty morning, run downstairs and get dressed in front of a big coal fire. Even in wartime we were never short of coal. My father had made it very clear to the coalman that Mum should never again be left without coal, after the time earlier in the year when he had come home on leave and found us without a fire. I'd like to think he told the coalman in a friendly way but I doubt it very much.

Mum was still very weak so, when she fell ill a couple of days before Christmas, the doctor ordered her to stay in bed. On Christmas Eve we were allowed to stay up a bit longer than usual. I was the one who went to the door to give the carol singers their pennies and, when it was time for bed, I did the usual chores, like putting hot plates into the bed. These plates were heavy steel plates that had been warmed in the fire side oven all day. When I had done this job and given everyone a warm drink, I had to undress my sister Ivy and brother Archie ready for bed and see that they got there. When that was done I mashed our usual cup of tea and sat down with Mum, but tonight, instead of telling me about the things that had happened around and about, she asked me if I could keep a secret. Of cause I said "Yes." She told me to go upstairs and find all the toys and presents that were hidden in her bedroom. She said that they would be all over the place. I was to look in cupboards, in drawers, in the wardrobe and behind it. It had been pulled out by Mrs. Kerkhoff before she had left earlier. I found all sorts of things in the oddest places. Every time I took some downstairs she would tell me that there were some more. I was getting pretty tired running up and down, but the tiredness went when I pulled the blankets back on the bed. There, laying as if sleeping, were two dolls. One just a bit bigger than the other. I knew instantly who they were for and I hoped I would get the bigger one. I took these very carefully downstairs. I put them at the side of Mum hoping she would say something that would confirm which was mine. "Is that the last of them Nancy?" I nodded but she asked me to go and check. On my return the dolls were gone. "Now Nancy, get me four pillow cases love." I only remembered filling two of them and putting them in the cupboard. When everything was done Mum said "Now Nancy, you must never tell the others what you know."

In the morning the other two woke me up saying that Father Christmas hadn't been yet. It seemed as if I had grown up overnight, because I didn't tell them what I knew. I just let them go downstairs to Mum. When I went down she was telling them that Father Christmas was too tired to climb the stairs this year so he left them in the cupboard.

When Mum saw me she said “Oh Nancy he left yours in the cupboard as well.” She gave me a knowing smile. I opened the pillow case and there she was. The biggest, loveliest doll I had ever seen. She was dressed in blue and that colour is still my favourite today. I got the breakfast over with then all the fun of Christmas started.

Although there was still a war on, the magic of Christmas was still there; Everybody kept coming in and out. Some people would bring presents and others would bring food and sometimes a bit of chocolate. Gran came and cooked the dinner and a couple of aunties stayed with us for that, but the one person we all wanted was not there. He would probably be on the high seas, somewhere off Scotland.

After the Christmas festivities were over and we had let in the new year, we settled down to 1945. It had been on everybody’s minds that, surely, the war would be over soon. The previous year, on June 6th, the landings at Normandy were a success never before seen. Over four thousand ships and small vessels were commandeered, not forgetting the vast amount of air power that was taking part in the biggest landing on French shores. On the Italian front, on June 4th, Rome was the first European capital to be liberated by the allies. Paris was liberated in August. The battle of Arnhem was in September and this was the only time we connected my father with any sort of danger, though I am sure there must have been many, many more times for him. He was due to be airlifted and dropped by parachute into Arnhem. Dad always had a policy of last in first out and this was to save his and a few of his friends lives. They were seated in the aircraft waiting for take off when an order came for volunteers. Dad was near the door, so was chosen along with a few other soldiers and, as history records, more than half the men perished on that raid. This was one of the few times Dad ever spoke about his time in the army.

It was around February when a letter came with an appointment to see a Mr. Hynes. Mum commented that she didn’t know this doctor, or dentist as the case may be. The appointment was still at the Royal Hospital, but we had to go to another department this time. When we got to the hospital we went to the reception. Mum had to bring baby Keith with us because she was breast feeding and she didn’t know how long we were going to be there. We were shown into a large waiting area with hundreds of wooden forms set outside doors that had numbers on them. We were told to sit outside number three. Soon my name was

called out and as we went through number three door the nurse said "Hello Nancy." She told Mum to sit in one chair and I was told to sit in the chair opposite the doctor. He was reading a paper when we went in, but as soon as I sat down he looked over his glasses at me and said "Hello Nancy Mallender. Thank you for coming to see me." Then he took his glasses off. I liked this man. He looked over at Mum and asked:
"How many children have you got Mrs. Mallender?"
"Four."
"Are the ones at home going to school?"
"Just one. Our Ivy is too young to go there yet."
"If she is old enough for the nursery would you like her to go?"
"Yes, I think so."
"Right, we'll see what we can do."
"Now young lady what can we do for you? Open your mouth for me and let me have a look."

Mr. Hynes turned out to be an eminent ear, nose and throat surgeon. He had just come out of the forces where he had been doing operations on casualties of the war. He was renowned for his work in plastic surgery, a very new technique used to rebuild shattered faces and repair the damage caused by burning. Here he was talking to me! "Now, how about if I give you a new nose? You will have to have a lot of patience and be brave because you will have to come into hospital quite a few more times. Will you do that for me?" By this time he had lifted me off the chair, stood me between his knees with my back to him and now he was talking to Mum again. "I'm sure we can do something for this little girl's face."

As we left, Mum made an appointment for the x-ray department. I was to have x-rays and photographs taken from every angle of my head. This was a new chapter in my life. I was never again to go into the children's hospital. From now on I would be going to a 'grown ups' hospital. The snow was still on the ground and I always seemed to have cold feet. However, we always went home to a nice warm house, except on wash days when we had to have the back door opened to let the steam out. The kitchen was always cold.

I had had the photographs and x-rays done and had been back to see Mr. Hynes. He said that he would send for me to come into hospital as soon as possible. It was the middle of March and Easter was just around the corner. Even in wartime, children still managed to get some chocolate eggs. People who had no children would willingly sell their sweet coupons or exchange them for food or other things. Mrs. Kerkhoff had an Easter egg mould. She would use cooking chocolate to make the eggs. It was somewhat of a triumph to get a good one out of three! If the chocolate broke in the process of being dislodged from the mould we would be allowed to eat some of the bits. I remember the Easter bonnet parades that marched around the streets. This parade was later to revert back to the big Easter parade that marched around the east end of Sheffield before the start of the war. After the war the big Easter parade did come back with as many as seventy floats or more. There were lorries and carts of every description. Some of the people pushed prams with grown up in them acting like babies and, at the head of the parade, there was always 'the fairy' or rather a man dressed as a fairy. Easter Monday was equal to Christmas in those days, but for now, only the bonnets.

I was still at Huntsman's Garden school. There wasn't a garden to be seen now, but it was named after the man who had the school built. Huntsman was a watchmaker who lived in Rotherham and later moved to Sheffield where he became a wealthy industrialist. He invented the 'cast' or 'crucible steel'. This fine steel was used to make parts for Huntsman's watches and other fine machinery. Huntsman noticed the squalor and the bad conditions his workers and their children lived in. So he built a school with gardens around it and, for his workers, he built houses with little gardens at the front and back. Some of these houses still stand today but the school has gone.

Just after Easter 1945 a letter came for me. It said that a bed had been reserved for me at the Fulwood Annex Hospital and that I was to have an operation on my nose. This was to be the start of a whole new experience for me. My association with this hospital was to last for over thirty eight years until its closure in the mid eighties.

On the way to the hospital we had to pass the Royal Hospital and pass near to the Children's hospital. It felt nice to be passing them. It was a long journey out into the country, past some very big, posh houses with big gardens and trees everywhere. Every time I did this journey it gave me the feeling that I was being transported into another world and I never tired of it. When we got off the bus at Fulwood church we walked on for a few metres, then turned into a drive that looked to be leading nowhere. It was a long, wide, steep drive leading down to a valley. We first saw the hospital roof tops. It appeared to have lots of chimneys. As we walked down the hill, the chimneys disappeared over the roof and then we saw the windows. We didn't realize we were approaching it from the back and, as a child, I was beginning to think how dark and small every thing was looking. We descended some stone steps into what looked like a back yard. Mum must have been wondering where we were going. I know I did and I wasn't too sure that I was going to like it here. We crossed the yard to a door that had a sign on it marked 'Office and all enquires'. Inside was the nicest surprise; It opened up into a long corridor, bright and cheerful, as was the nurse who met us. My confidence was coming back.

We were told to sit on some chairs outside an office. I noticed that all the utility rooms, such as the bathrooms, toilets and store rooms, were all down the left side of the corridor. On the right were all the wards. Like all children I was inquisitive, so I walked a few steps away from my mother to walk down the corridor. On the left, I saw it: 'Operating Theatre'. I had seen these two words often enough to know what they meant. So I went back to my Mum and sat on her knee.

The office door opened and a tall lady came out. She wore a navy blue dress with a silver buckled belt. The dress had long sleeves with white cuffs and on her head she wore a lovely little white cap. She was like no other nurse I had seen. She turned out to be the Matron of the hospital. She smiled and with one hand stretched towards Mum and, looking down at me, she said "Please come in Mrs. Mallender, Nancy." After the preliminaries of booking in were done, Matron took us to a ward. It looked more like a posh hotel room than a ward. There were six beds in the room and, opposite the door we had just come through, there was a French window leading out on to a raised terrace that overlooked a beautiful and well kept garden. This was to be my home for the next six weeks. Matron introduced us to the ward sister and then took her leave as a nurse came over to tell us the routine of the hospital and the visiting times. When all this was done it was time for Mum to leave. I was allowed to take her to the outside door where we had come in. I tried not to cry. After all, I was a big girl now and I was in a new hospital, but the tears came just the same and Mum, brave lady that she was, just waved and was gone.

The nurse and I went back to the ward. There were five ladies in the ward and they all became my aunty somebody or other. I was to have a lifetime affection for this hospital and it's staff.

When I awoke the next morning it was to the sound of birds and, out of all the sounds, the crow was the loudest. There seemed to be millions of these big black birds, but as the sun caught the shine on their feathers, they became a deep petrol blue colour. I would watch them for hours. Living down Attercliffe it was rare to hear birds through the noise of the factories. This profusion of sound was beautiful, even if it was only five-thirty in the morning. I was to lay, listening to this sound on many, many more occasions. At six-thirty the nurse came in with the tea trolley. The birds had quietened down by now and the ladies, after their 'good mornings' had been said, laid in quiet thought sipping their tea. Something told me not to break this special silence.

Fulwood Annex Hospital was administered by the Sheffield Royal Hospital. The unit was originally the Zachory Merton Convalescent Home. Zachory Merton gave some money to the Royal Hospital after the death of his wife in 1930. With this money the Hospital built the convalescent home. It was opened in 1938 and became part of the National Health Service in 1948. One half of the building specialized in neuromedicine, later becoming the Burns Unit. The remaining area was for the new, and still experimental, plastic surgery specializing in facial disfigurements and facial prosthesis. I would get to know every part of this hospital in due course, but for now, like the rest of my 'aunties' we were drinking our tea.

For the rest of that day I was left to get to know everybody and where the essential places were, such as the bathroom, dining room and the places where I could and couldn't go. On the corridor I could go up to the exit door but I couldn't go beyond it. I was very intrigued to know what was round the corner at the top of the corridor. It would be four more years before I found out. I felt as if I was on a great new adventure.

The next day I was woken up in the usual way and was allowed to get dressed in my own clothes. After breakfast I was told that I was going to see Mr. Hynes. A nurse took me by the hand down the long corridor. Near the end we came to a door marked 'E.N.T.' In my little world this was short for enter, but as my knowledge grew I realized it meant Ear, Nose and Throat department. Behind the door were narrow steps leading down. These steps were no wider than our cellar steps at home. I didn't like them at home, but I disliked these even more. I wanted to go back to the ward. At the bottom was another door that lead into a small waiting-room with painted brick walls. Our wait today was only for a moment, but I was to wait in here for many, many years to come; through childhood, young adult-hood and well into being a married women. The door opened and there he was. He took my hand as he lead me into the surgery and then he lifted me up into the 'big chair'.

The run up to my first operation at Fulwood was very much the same as always; People asking me questions and nobody telling me anything, except that there was one highlight in that week of waiting. I got my first ride in an ambulance. I had to go to the Royal Hospital to have some photographs taken. I was photographed from each side, full front, from the top of my head and then from the chin up. The last one was a bit scary because, in those days, no one bothered to explain what was going to happen. So out of the blue and in an abrupt fashion I was laid down on a table, told to lift my chin as high as I could and try to look at the wall above my head. In this position I saw two light bulb flashers under my chin and two more above my head. From here I could see the hairs up the photographer's nose. I wanted to laugh, but I daren't. I told my nurse on the way back and she started laughing.

Being new to the hospital I didn't know the routine on operating days. The day began with a nurse inadvertently nudging the bed when she put the 'nil by mouth' sign over the top of the bed. At least that part was the same. I was woken up again and taken to the bathroom where I had a bath, but not before I had had an enema. Thankfully this practice was phased out, but in those days it was something they thought had to be done. After the bath I was put back into bed in a white gown that was far too big for a seven year old girl like me. Everything that happened in the run up to an operation was starting to happen. The screens were put around the bed. Another white gown was put at the bottom of the bed, again ten sizes too big. The ladies seemed to have gone away. It was quiet, except for the two that were in bed and they were talking in whispers. I tried to listen but couldn't hear what they were whispering about. They had been told to keep as quiet as they could.

After a while a nurse came and gave me a pre-med injection that still hurt. She sat and talked to me for a while and, as she talked, I felt

The Royal Hospital's Fulwood Annexe

safe and relaxed. This had never happened in the children's hospital. In there I felt scared, alone and bewildered by it all. Later I heard the trolley being manoeuvred into place by my bed. The screens were pulled back and I was put onto it. I woke up to reality five days later.

My recollections of this time are very dim. I was told that I had developed pneumonia after the operation. My breathing and airways were very restricted due to the work done on my nose and, apparently, I was worrying everybody to death for a few days, wondering if I would make it back to the land of the living. When I did finally come round it was to see Mum. She was surrounded by flowers and cards people had sent to me and the presents made it look like Christmas. I had to stay in bed for a long time. My aunties were very good to me, getting things that were out of reach for me and telling me stories.

In that critical week Mum came to see me every day. I found out years later that, due to lack of funds, she would walk the first two and a half miles to Sheffield town, then catch the tram to Fulwood church. Going back she would ride to town then walk the rest. She was never allowed to stay more than a few hours with me before she had to leave again. When the crisis was over it was back to the usual five visits a week.

As I laid in my bed I used to wonder what I looked like. I had got a 'new nose' so why, when I asked for a mirror, would no one would give me one? I wasn't allowed out of bed so I couldn't look into a bathroom mirror. I must have been a pain the neck over this mirror thing because the sister came to me. She told me I was not looking my best at the moment because of all the swelling in my face. She went on to say that I was very bruised around the eyes and that was why my eyes were almost shut. In fact, I looked like a bashed up panda if the truth be known, and that would be to put it mildly. She went on to explain that I had got some new bone graft in my nose and that lifted the bridge and lengthened the nose at the same time. This meant that the skin had to be stretched to cover the new fashioned nose, plus a new piece had to be introduced to separate the nostril passages. So, all in all, it had been a big job for such a little nose.

When the sister came on the next day, she came into the ward and I saw that she was holding a mirror. She put the screens around the bed and then sat down beside me. It was almost two weeks since the operation. I had been having my mouth and nose cleaned twice a day with some fluid that would sting like mad, so I still had a lot of soreness around that area. I had to have a mouthwash after every meal. The meal would usually be strained broth or creamed soup and always tepid warm. I had to drink by a feeder cup and I couldn't have anything that was very cold, such as ice-cream. So now, here I was with the sister and a mirror. She put the mirror on the bed beside me. "Do you really want to see yourself Nancy?" she asked. I must have nodded. She went on to remind me of yesterday's conversation and assured me that it would get better and that the swelling would go down as it had been doing for the last few days.

She then put the mirror in my hand. I remember wanting to give it back to her for her to show me my face. I now knew I was scared at what I was going to see. As I lifted the mirror it showed the top of my head. As I lowered it the full realization hit me. It was awful; This was not me, I was little, not big and was funny colours. I wanted to be normal. I recall that I cried uncontrollably for a long time. When I had calmed down the nurse, who had replaced the sister, asked me if I would like to get out of bed for a change. I was put into a wheelchair and taken towards the door. I didn't want to go out, not today, so I was left in the room to talk to some of the ladies who were left in their beds. I soon forgot the traumas of that morning.

The next day, after breakfast, I was told that I had to get up and have a little walk around. I had seen what had happened to the other ladies after they had stayed in bed for a while and I had been in bed for longer than any of them. I was not looking forward to it at all. As predicted, after breakfast, two nurses came. They sat me on the edge of the bed to put my slippers on. I began to feel sick. I told them I wanted to go back to bed, but my plea fell on deaf ears. I was hoisted up on to my feet. I knew my feet were on the ground but it felt like a floating sensation. I tried to put one foot in front of the other. The ladies began to see the funny side of it and their laughter became contagious. In the end we were all laughing together as the nurses lifted me back into bed for a rest. They had to repeat the exercise several times before I was confident to walk on my own again and then I had to go around holding the furniture like a baby would do. I got my first opportunity to go to the bathroom on my own. I could just see into the mirror if I stood on my tip toes. I had a strapping of plaster across my nose, but that didn't stop me seeing and confirming what I had already seen before. I still wasn't convinced that I would ever be normal again. Just then, one of my 'aunties' came in and caught me. I thought she was going to shout at me, but she just said "Give it time love, give it time." I wondered for a long time after that how did she know what I was thinking? The rest of my stay in hospital was pleasant. When any of the staff had some free time they would take me, and one ore two others, out into the grounds. Sometimes we would go for a walk around Forge Dam. This area was adjacent to the gardens of the annex.

Mr. Hynes had been to see me at intervals while I was ill, but today I had to go and see him in the E.N.T. department. I was introduced to a Mr. Raynor. Mr. Hynes told me that Mr. Raynor would be taking care of me and my teeth from now on and that he knew all about me and that I was not to worry. This new man in my life was not very tall, but he had a nice smile. He had little lines at the sides of his eyes. I would be looking at these eyes for the next eighteen years. I sat in the chair waiting for them to finish talking. The nurse was filling a cup with water. As she put it at the side of me the two most important people in my life came back over to me. It was Mr. Hynes who asked if I would like to try my teeth in today. I hadn't worn them for over four weeks. I remember feeling a little unsure about this, but I nodded anyway. With this signal Mr. Raynor went into a side room and when he came back he was holding a white enamel bowl. He took the lid off and there were my teeth. Now in my young mind I just couldn't figure out how he came to have them. He must have seen the querying look on my face because as he took them out of the bowl he said "I've been saving them for you Nancy. Now open your mouth wide." Mr. Hynes was watching as he gently put them in. It felt as if I was wearing them for the first time again. I was being told to close my lips together, but not my teeth just yet. Then Mr. Raynor said "Now very gently close your teeth together." As I did this I felt the sharp pain at the top of my mouth and tears sprung to my eyes. Not because I was crying, it just made my eyes water. Mr. Raynor quickly took the teeth out again. He reached for the drill, then he started to take some of the height off the top of the palate. He rinsed it under the tap, then did the whole procedure of putting them back into my mouth again. It was still too painful to wear them. On the third try, I decided that was going to say they were all right even if they still hurt a bit, but to my surprise, I was telling the truth when I said "No, they don't hurt now."

Back in the ward I was the star of the show. My 'aunties' were saying "Come on Nancy give us a smile." I must have gone around the hospital with a permanent smile on my face for the rest of the day.

Another week was to pass with another photographic session and then I could go home. However, now I didn't want to go home. I felt safe here. Yes, I wanted to see my brothers and sisters, but I didn't want to leave the seclusion of this place. When my mother came for me it must have hurt her a lot to hear me say I didn't want to leave the hospital. I couldn't explain the turmoil that was going on in my mind. A lot of what was happening at this time I don't recall. I can't remember much about my return to school, but what I do remember is being the eldest in the class now. Because my year had moved on and the powers that be had decided, in their wisdom, that it would be better to leave me in the year that I had left eight weeks ago, rather than let me be with the few friends I had made and hope that I would catch up with them in the school program. But no, here I was playing mother at school now, as well as at home.

I was still not allowed to take part in any physical exercises, ball games of any sort, or any other games which put me at risk. All through this period it was never explained to me why I couldn't take part. I just assumed that I wasn't good enough at anything. I was left ignorant of the true facts, with an inferior complex that was growing and continued to grow until I was fifteen years old. At this age things started to change for me in a big way and that included my name, but for now it was play time in the school yard.

CHAPTER 3

IN DARKEST HOURS GOD SMILES

On May 8th 1945 the war was finally over. I remember everyone was happy. Strangers greeted each other with the same question "When will he be home?" or "It won't be long now before he's home." Everywhere you went there was a party atmosphere. I was too young to know the real meaning of all this hilarity, but I know even to someone as young as I was, it felt better than the tensions of war.

The blinds to the windows came down and there were more people on the streets. Shop windows were starting to stay decorated and lit up at nights, there was a growing air of contentment everywhere and, of course, there were the street parties. For these parties the food was laid on in abundance. Where it came from, no-one asked and it was definite that no-one was telling either. We just ate it and had a grand and glorious time. It was at these times that I wished our Dad could be here, but it was not to be because, unknown to Mum or anybody, he had been commissioned to stay in London to search for unexploded bombs. In the months that followed the end of the war we saw our Dad more often, but he still didn't tell Mum what he was doing down in London. It was a long time after he got home for good that he told Mum the truth about the job he had been doing.

We were getting to the close of this very eventful year. I had some new teeth and had been back to see Mr. Hynes. He was satisfied with the progress I was making and suggested that I might be getting ready for my next operation. This one would be at the back of my throat. The intention was to give me an uvula. This is a small fleshy appendage suspended from the back of the palate over the back of the tongue.

This would enable me to pronounce words such as 'ringing, queen, queuing, sinking, and king', all guttural sounds made with the back of the throat, but it was going to be an unknown area. I would be one of the first, and certainly the youngest, to have this done. The dangers were many; I could choke and have to be rushed back to the theatre to have the whole thing reversed, the newly grafted tissue may be rejected and it may not even work in the way it was expected to. It could hinder what little speech power I had and so I may still have to have the whole thing reversed. When Mum had listened to everything Mr. Hynes had to say, he told us to go home and think about it. It must have been a miserable time for Mum to have to make such a decision. Dad took very little part at these times, telling Mum that whatever she thinks is best is all right with him.

The start of 1946 brought the first New Year of peace for six years. Our Dad had been home for Christmas and had gone back, without the assistance of the military police. It was just after this festive time that a letter came from the Royal Hospital. Usually Mum wasn't too bothered about letters from the hospital, but she knew this time it was going to be a risky operation. When I had my nose done she came to see me and she was convinced that they had 'done it'. They had made me look like a monkey and our neighbour, Kerkhoff, had had the job of convincing her that it would be all right when the swelling had gone down and, no doubt, she would have the job of convincing Mum that she had made the right decision what ever the outcome was. The thought must have weighed heavily on both their minds that they had nearly lost me once.

We had to go and see Mr. Hynes at the Sheffield Royal Hospital. We were shown into the same number three door and he was sat there waiting for us. Mum was talking to him for a long time. A lot of what was said went right over an eight year old's head. I didn't know what fifty-fifty meant but it was said on more than one occasion. Mum started to cry, smiled at me and said "Do you want to talk a bit better than you do now Nancy?" I thought it was a silly question because I thought I spoke all right now. Mr. Hynes was sat opposite us. He took my hand and stood me between his knees. He always put me in this position when he had anything serious to say to me.

"Look at me Nancy. Say kings."

"ing."

"Say Queen."

“ween.”
“Would you like to say Q and K and ings like everyone else does?” My answer was the usual nod of the head. So Mum and I left the hospital to await our next appointment for Fulwood Annex.

It came in February. The snow had been threatening for a few days. The few flakes of snow we had seen were quickly washed away with the icy rain of the morning. Mum read the letter very quickly then put it on the mantle shelf saying “you’re going to the hospital on Sunday morning Nancy.”

The day before we were walking down the drive of the hospital it had been snowing heavily for most of the day. Now I had never seen snow as white as it was at Fulwood. Living down Attercliffe the snow was dirtied very quickly with the soot and grime from the works and the house chimneys and the heat from the factories soon melted the snow into dirty muddy puddles. Mum and I just stood and looked out over the valley. The white fields were separated by hedges that were weighted down with snow and in one or two corners of the fields we could see cows huddled together trying to keep warm. The crows looked blacker now against the background of white. I remember thinking, it looks just like a Christmas card.

It felt as if I was coming home when I was taken to ward six again. The sister on duty was the same and two of the nurses were still there. I was sorry not to see any of my ‘auntie’s’, but I realized that they would have got better and gone home. In the next few days there was the usual round of tests and questions. Swabs were taken from my throat, people were writing things down and saying very little to me about what was going to happen. I remember looking out at the snow and wishing I could go out and play with it. I couldn’t stop looking out of the ward windows. Just to look at the snow was a wonder. I was beginning to notice the finer things in life, like the foot prints of the birds where someone had cleared a space for them and the snow had lightly covered it again. It was while I was looking at this postcard scene that I saw my first robin, a bird you would definitely not see in heavily industrialized Attercliffe. The snow had fallen heavily again overnight so there were a lot of nurses who could not get home. At last I got my wish. Some of the off-duty nurses took a few of the children out into the grounds. We built the biggest snowman I had ever seen. In fact it scared me a little bit when I saw him out there in the dark. He seemed to glow. Being a child, I didn't realize it was the light from the ward reflecting off the pure white snow.

When the traffic started to get through again Mum came to see me. A nurse took Mum and I to the E.N.T. department where Mr. Hynes was waiting for us. We were shown into a little office instead of the surgery and this change of routine unnerved me a bit. Mr. Hynes and Mum talked about the operation. He was telling her "It would take more than one operation to get it right. It may even take three, but we're hoping it will only be two." Mum shook hands with him and as we left he hooked my chin in his hand and said "I'll be seeing you later young lady."

A few days after this meeting I was on my way to the operating theatre again. I woke up with a very sore throat. It was very early in the morning. I could hear the familiar noise of the crows. You couldn't call it a song, it was just a noise. I heard the sound of scurrying feet to my bed. A nurse was saying "Hello, you've decided to join us at last." The next thing I remember was a stranger walking up the ward with Mum. He was the doctor. He was telling Mum that the exploratory operation had given them good results and that they were satisfied that the main operation could go ahead. I asked Mum what he meant. She explained that this operation was to find out whether it was safe to carry on with the big one, and that it was. If it was only a little operation I had then why was my throat hurting so much? Mum explained that they had taken a sample of skin from the roof of my mouth, but neither of us ever found out why this had been done. A few days later I was allowed to go home.

Easter came around and in the shops were chocolate Easter eggs wrapped up in silver paper. I was too young to remember the last time I had seen them in the shops, never mind being wrapped like this. On Easter Sunday we all got an Easter egg and none of them were cracked or broken.

It was late summer when I was once again in hospital. The grounds of the hospital were looking lovely, with the late summer flowers still in full bloom. I had seen Mr. Hynes and he had told me that this was going to be one of the big ones. I was in a different ward this time. Ward ten was long with windows on all three sides. It was like a finger sticking out from the main body of the hospital. The hospital was an 'E' shape, without the middle bit of the 'E'. This ward was at one of the ends. It had five beds down each side. At the top was the nurse's table with a table lamp on it. This lamp bathed the whole table in a pool of yellow light when the main ward was in darkness. At first I didn't like the ghostlike appearance of the nurse sat at the table, so I would turn my back to it when I lay in bed.

The views from the ward were better than ward six, but there was no door to get out into the garden so we had to go through ward six and out through the French windows. In the middle of the ward was a large table where we could play table games until it was time for a meal, when we would have to clear everything away. It was here that I learned how to set a table for breakfast, dinner and supper. Tea was always taken in bed when the visitors had gone. It was always policy that all the patients should be in bed whenever doctors or visitors were in the ward. Even if you were bursting to go the toilet you had to wait until the ward was cleared, then the mad dash would begin either to be first on the buzzer for a bed pan or first at the toilets. The visiting times had been increased considerably to half an hour every evening, with another hour Saturday and Sunday afternoons.

The day I had been dreading dawned. I went for my bath and the enemas were still being done. Now I was tucked up in my bed just watching the activity around me. With the countless days I had already spent in hospital I had begun to notice certain routines of the working days in the wards. I noticed that in the mornings, with the exception of Sundays, all the beds would be moved from one side of the ward to the other. The cleaners would then clean down the empty side of the ward, push the beds back into place, then repeat the same routine all over again down the opposite side. This was done with the exception of beds with patients waiting to go down to theatre. Then they just swept and dusted around them. I was hoping that they would move my bed, but no, the events of that day were made definite when they left me where I was.

I was given the pre-med injection and, for some reason, I was scared. I think I had picked up on the vibes that this operation was going to be special and, as I have said before, they didn't say a lot to a little girl like me. The screens had been pulled around my bed and, for a while, I was left with my thoughts. A nurse came around the screens. She could see I was upset and asked "What's up Nancy?" With this show of sympathy I started to cry and replied "I'm scared." She reminded me that I had already had lots of operations and this one should be no different to the others. Her arms were round my shoulders and she gave me a little squeeze as she said "I'll be back in a minute", and sure enough she was. She had been to get a teddy bear that I had adopted. She told me not to let any one see him and that he was to be our secret. She stayed with me until the trolley arrived to take me and Ted to the theatre.

When I came round I had tubes disappearing up my nose and into my arms. I was told that I had to lay flat on my back and not to try to sit up. It felt like an eternity that I was laid like this. Days turned into nights and nights turned in to days. I could suck ice-cubes and I could sip cool water, but this would inevitably come back down my nose because, once again, I was without teeth and I still had a cleft palate. I was injected at regular intervals and, in those days, there were no throw away syringes. All the needles would be used a multitude of times before being declared blunt. This latter statement was only evident when the hole it left was a wound, rather than a small puncture. The phrase "I hope it's sharp" was regularly used as a plea, rather than a joke.

In the first few days after the operation no-one spoke to me by way of a question, so I did no talking. I had been moved to the end of the ward. The bottom of my bed was in line with the nurses table so that when the lights went out in the ward and the table light was on, I could not turn over away from the shadows on the ceiling, I remember being frightened of the different shapes of the nurses head and the monstrous sizes it would take on when she stood up. The shadow was a giant and I would close my eyes. I could not tell any one about my fears because I was not allowed to speak.

The screens were always drawn down one side of the bed so that I could see the table but not the rest of the ward. I could see the other patients when they passed the end of my bed, going out of or coming in to the ward. Then they would only wave or mime hello. I felt very isolated, especially when I could hear laughter around the meal table. I was told that no visitors would be coming for a few days, so here I was virtually on my own.

When the day came for the tubes to be removed from my nose it was not a happy one. I remember being sick and feeling very ill. I could feel something running down the back of my throat. I could hardly breath and every so often a mask was held over my face. This eased my breathing problem, but after a time it was taken away again. This situation went on for a few hours. I was told that it was touch and go for a while. It was as if I had gone into shock. Eventually I did start to breath on my own.

I woke up to see my mother and grandmother at the side of the bed and the screens had gone. It was a kind of relief to be able to look down the ward again and wave to people. I still wasn't allowed to sit up but, with the help of an extra pillow, I could see a bit more of the ward. I was surprised to see new people in the ward and sad that some of my friends had gone home. I couldn't talk to anybody because I had lost my voice. I was quickly reassured that it would come back soon, but without my palate I couldn't speak anyway.

It was about a week after the operation that I was allowed to put my little front teeth back in and this time it felt normal, but just a little sore at the back of my throat. At least I could drink without turning into a human waterfall. When the drip in my arm was removed, I was told I could eat normal food from now on. My first meal was a bowl of watery soup with very small pieces of vegetables in it. It was very painful and hard for me to get it past my throat and after two or three tries it ended in tears. The nurse was pleading with me to try harder and saying "If you don't eat you won't be able to go home" but, try as I might, it was just too painful for me.

The next day Mr. Hynes came to see me. He had obviously been told that I was struggling. He came into the ward and just stood there looking at me with his 'what have we here' look on his face. He sat on the side of the bed and said "Nancy, I know you are thinking that the pain will never stop, but it will. Your voice will come back then you will be able to speak normally again, but it will take time. So will you try just a little bit harder to eat as much food as you can? When you have eaten your meals you can have as much ice-cream as you want, but only if you eat your meals first." So with my trust in his words I began to eat. I must have been given every variety of soup that there was in the world. I noticed that the very small vegetables were becoming bigger as time went on. The food went down very painfully at first, but then, as if by magic, I began to notice that it wasn't hurting quite so much.

I had been in hospital for approximately two weeks when I was told a speech therapist was coming to see me. When she came into the ward she reminded me of a teacher I didn't like. She asked me all sorts of questions and if I answered her with a nod she got cross and said she wanted a verbal answer and not a nod. At first I didn't know the meaning of the word 'verbal', but I knew what she meant when she said "Just talk to me and don't nod your head." I was right, I didn't like her very much. After a few of her visits Mr. Hynes came to see me and he had me saying "king, queen, squash." I could see his smile getting broader and broader every time I said a new word. He then said "Tomorrow Nancy I am going to bring two people to see you. Will you speak to them for me?" My head responded in reply "And when your Mum comes, I want you to speak to her in your best voice and if you make a good job of it I may let you go home."

The next day Mum and Mr. Hynes with his two friends came in to the ward. He looked at me and said "Well?" I said in my best voice "Hello Mum. I can say queen and king now." Her smile spoke volumes to anyone in the know, but to me as a little girl, I thought that I had just done a good job and had pleased everyone. I was allowed to go home a few days later.

After I was discharged from the hospital I had to attend a speech therapy clinic three times a week on Mondays, Wednesdays and Fridays. The clinic was on Newbold lane. It was a large Victorian town house, but it still looked like a mansion to me. As we entered through the large front door I could see the ceiling in the hall was very high. Mum and I were asked to wait here for a moment. There was a wide stone staircase leading to the upper floor. I always wanted to go up them, but I never did get the chance. We were shown into a large room with a beautiful bay window. Everything about this place seemed to be on a grand scale. I think it was because I wasn't used to anything more than a two-up two-down and very basic needs in life.

Here we were introduced to Miss Pollitt. The moment I set eyes on her I liked her. I think it may have been relief that she wasn't the speech therapist I had seen at the hospital. Miss Pollitt was a very caring person who got the best she could from her clients, but sometimes all she got from me were tears of frustration. It was at these times she would put her arm around me and say "Don't worry Nancy. It's not that important yet. Now shall we try again?" She hadn't got the technology that there is today. The things she used were feathers, paper, white table tennis balls and balloons. She would get me to blow the feather while she moved it away from my mouth to see how far away she could get before it stopped waving about. The paper was used for drawing shapes of the mouth. The 'oo' shape was different from the 'a' shape, and so on. The paper also had another purpose; It was placed in a pile and I had to see how much of it I could blow off the top at one go. The tennis ball would be held to my lips. I would then have to suck in and see how long I could hold it for without using my hands. The balloon was a sound producer. Miss Pollitt used this for making vibrations by holding it to my lips while I made the sounds of 'ms', 'bs' and 'os', etc. It was work to her but it was good fun to me.

Going to the speech clinic three times a week must have put a great burden on my mother's already heavily laden shoulders. Dad was out of the army but wasn't ready to take on the roll of a full time father yet. Mum was pregnant again with her sixth child.

In this year, 1946, there were a lot of changes going on. These changes affected every one; young and old, rich and poor. The war had stopped and so had the army pay. So if a man couldn't find work his family suffered a lot of poverty and hardship. My father got work almost immediately, but then he would trade his wages for drink. His liking for the beer grew with his distaste for the war. Every week Mum always managed to get hold of some of the wages before he reached the pub.

Dad was turning into a Jekyll and Hyde character. I was almost nine years old at the time. It was hard for me to understand my own feelings without having this new father in our lives. He was new to us in that we hardly knew him before he had to go to war. So here he was, shouting at Mum and telling us what to do and if we didn't do it immediately we would know about it. Where was the happy soldier who used to come home on leave, bringing presents for us, kissing Mum and making her laugh? Our situation wasn't unique. It happened to so many men and their families. A lot of marriages never survived the after-war reunions.

My brother, Michael, was born in October as I was nine. On November 5th we had the biggest bonfire I had ever seen. It was as if the folks were burning all the contents of their homes. I saw chairs, tables and cupboards, old rugs and lino. It was as if people wanted a new start after the war and the bonfire gave them that chance.

I remember this year as the year I grew up. I learned how to avoid my father when he was in one of his moods. I kept my brothers and sisters out of the way by taking them for long walks and we only went into the house if tea was ready or if it was time for bed. After tea Dad would fall asleep in his chair and woe betide anyone who woke him up. It was at these times when we would reduce ourselves into fits of laughter, by imitating Dad's snoring and the way that he laid in his chair. Mum would try and chastise us for it, but there was always that little smile on her face. When the hilarity got too much we were shown the door double quick before Dad woke up.

I don't remember much about my last weeks at Huntsman's Gardens School, but I do remember the feeling of relief when I was told I was going to go to a new school. It would be after the Christmas holidays.

I was still attending speech therapy clinic, but the visits were down to once a week now. I had learned how to use my 'new' throat and how not to talk down through my nose. I was taught how to use the muscles in my throat to direct my voice over my tongue and through my lips. I was using open vowel sounds more clearly and my speech in general had improved one hundred percent. With the speech lessons came elocution and, though I did not realize it at the time, I was beginning to speak in a more precise manner. Now I couldn't get away with it for long before someone would be saying 'Hark at her. Who does she think she is?' I quickly learned that to keep friends you joined them in every way and this meant keeping inside their language barriers. So, now I had two speaking worlds; I had to speak nicely for Miss Pollitt and remember where I was when I was at home in Attercliffe.

My new school was to be Maud Maxfield's school for the deaf. It was then on East Bank Road, Sheffield. It was relocated in 1951 to Bents Green, Ringinglow Road. It is still a mystery to me why I was sent to this school at all. None of the pupils could speak to me. I often had to turn to the teachers for help to tell me what was being said by them and even then I would feel guilty. I was not allowed to use sign language. This form of communication was not encouraged so you would be punished if you were caught using it. Unless I was prepared to break the rules and take a chance there wasn't much opportunity to use this sort of communication either. But on the way home on the bus or tram the sign language was very much in evidence. It was while I was at this school that I was to be accused, yet again, of something I hadn't done. However, it was very serious this time.

The history of this school is very interesting; Approximately eighty years ago most deaf children in Sheffield were being educated in residential institutions in Doncaster, Manchester, Derby or Leeds. These were charitable foundations dependent on the rising tide of Victorian philanthropy. In 1919 a small group of deaf children were being educated in Sheffield in a house in the Crookes area.

At this time Maud Maxfield was on the Sheffield Education Committee. She was untiringly working on behalf of the handicapped children in the city. She was also Deputy Chairman of the Special Schools Section. In 1921 Miss Maxfield persuaded the Sheffield Authority to buy the former home of Mr. Talbot Wilson at East Hill, Norfolk Park. This was adapted to take eighty deaf children. Although it was near the centre of the city, the new school was in open space with gardens and fields around it. In September 1922, the Maud Maxfield school opened under the headship of Mary Grace Wilkins with eight members of staff to help her. The first pupils were aged between five and six years, with varying degrees of deafness. Many had been taught in the institutions by the manual methods. It was a mammoth task to mould this heterogeneous group into a semblance of order. Miss Wilkins was a good teacher of speech, and lip reading was a very high priority. Many of the pupils from the institutions had never been taught lip-reading. Under successive head teachers the school maintained its position as one of the leaders of oral teaching in the country, established by the efforts of Miss Wilkins and her pioneering staff. Maud Maxfield school was one of the war casualties in the Sheffield 'blitz' in 1940. When the children arrived back from evacuation they were taught in long wooden huts. I was one of the children taught in these huts.

Christmas came and went and the New Year meant a fresh start. We saw the laughing soldier in my dad again, but sadly it didn't last. After the holidays we didn't see much of him at all. He would work long twelve hour shifts, seven days a week. He would come home, have his tea then fall asleep while reading the evening newspaper. Then at seven o'clock he and Mum would get ready to go out, leaving us with an aunt or neighbour for the evening. This became a regular pattern.

The first day back to school arrived. I was up with my brothers and sisters, helping Mum to get them ready and giving out the breakfasts. I went with Mum when she took them to school. It felt strange not to be going in with them any more. I felt sort of outside the family for a while. When they were safely inside Mum and I went shopping. I had a new dress "For a new school" as my Mother put it.

The next morning was the usual family scramble for the sink and the breakfast table and Mum left the baby with Kerkhoff. Mum and I left the others at school again and now it was my turn. Mum and I caught the tram to Norfolk Bridge. I was told to take notice of where I was going because I would be doing this on my own one day. We got off the tram and crossed the busy main road with a warning from Mum that if I was on my own, I was to ask someone to take me across. This was the main artery road to Rotherham. Our next part of the journey was on one of the few single deck buses that were around at that time. We arrived at the school and were shown into a small office at one end of one of the huts.

The head teacher was Miss Elliott. She was a very motherly person but I didn't like her office. On one wall there was a large picture frame full of butterflies. I was horrified when I realized that they weren't painted but stuck onto the board with a pin through every one. Although their colours were beautiful I could only think that they were all dead. I didn't like the sight of them at all so, whenever I had to go into this office, I would avoid looking at them. Mum and I were taken to my first classroom. It looked too small for the number of pupils that were in it. I had been used to a large classroom with a very high ceiling. This one seemed very small with a low ceiling.

When my Mother left me I was so frightened. I think at that moment I didn't like her or anybody else for making me go to this 'strange' school. I remember feeling very lonely and that I was not wanted. I didn't fit into this category of school. I protested very strongly every morning at having to go. My thoughts were 'My parents don't even care about me, or how I feel.' It must have been a trying time for them, especially for Mum. Eventually I did settle down and in a few weeks I was travelling to school on my own. My Mother would ask the conductor to put me off at the appropriate stop. I used to wonder what would happen if he forgot, though I soon found out. Shortly I remembered for myself and I would get off at the right place. I was very proud of myself for being so clever, but I never told anyone because I thought that the conductor would get into trouble. I didn't want that because he was a nice man. So this was the thinking of a very protective nine years old girl!

At school I was beginning to learn how to lip read along with basic communication skills, such as eye contact when I needed to speak to someone. I was making friends and feeling a lot happier. So many faces from this school I remember, but it's sad that my memory robs me of their names.

It was at around this time that something very odd started to happen. My palate began to feel as if it was being pushed down from the roof of my mouth and this caused it to become very loose. I would clean my teeth every morning and find that the fit was getting worse. So, an appointment was made for me to see Mr. Raynor, the dental technician. As he examined my mouth with the usual umm's and are's, he was looking at me from time to time. I was getting the feeling that all was not well. He tapped on what I thought was bone, but I heard the sound that you get when someone taps on your teeth. It was then that I realized I was growing teeth at the front of my mouth. I had visions of never having to wear dentures again. Mr. Raynor was saying "I think Mr. Hynes should take a look at this Nancy."

Our next visit to Fulwood soon put paid to any hopes I had of getting rid of the dentures. In fact, Mr. Hynes explained to me why I could not let the teeth grow any more. He said "Nancy, as much as I would like to let you keep the teeth, I can't. You see, all teeth should grow straight up or down from the top of your mouth. These teeth are growing across. So, when they meet in the middle, they will start to break and maybe give you a lot of pain. As you know your gums don't meet in the middle as they should and the two teeth are growing from the sides of the gap." He could see how disappointed I was so, he took me in his arms and gave me a hug and said "Never mind. When you have had them out Mr. Raynor will make you some lovely new teeth and they will be a lot nicer than the funny old things that are growing at the moment." With that, the arrangements were made for me to have the teeth out by way of a small operation. It took me a long time to get over the disappointment. I really did think that I was going to be like everybody else with my own front teeth.

After the operation to have the teeth removed, I spent a few days at home waiting for the swelling to go down. I couldn't speak without my false ones in, so it was another enforced holiday. This time , however, I did look forward to going back to Maud Maxfield School.

There was only one thing I dreaded at this school and that was the 'Zone' room. This was another wooden building at the top of a small hill but still in the grounds. We had to pass the old house that had been the first Maud Maxfield School. It had been severely damaged by the bombs in the Sheffield blitz and now it was eerie to see it all boarded up with corrugated iron from the old air raid shelters. It had big pieces of wood across the large front door. As we passed the big, rambling Victorian house we would tell our own stories about the people who used to live there and, of course, it was haunted. The Wilsons must have turned in their graves if they were listening to some of the tales that were being told.

The zone room was laid out with a semicircular bench-type table. On this was about a dozen sets of earphones. In front of this table was another table with electronic devices that were used to monitor all the sound levels that would come through the earphones. These sounds could be soft, fuzzy, loud or sharp. My sounds were always too loud and I would always come out of that lesson with fuzzy hearing and really afraid that, one day, I might go deaf. When I tried to tell them I wasn't deaf I received a scolding for my pains, so I didn't try that any more. I just used to put my index fingers up between the earphones and my ears and pressed the sound out that way. I now have two phobias in my life; I can not tolerate anyone standing in front of me and the other was born in the zone room. I cannot now wear earplugs or earphones of any kind without feeling sick.

I have one thing to thank the zone room for. It was here that I learned to appreciate good classical music. We had to listen to a piece of music and tap out the different rhythms. The Blue Danube Waltz, The Post Horn Gallop and Ravel's Bolero became my life time favourites.

Easter had come and gone and Whitsuntide was fast approaching. Every year, at this time, Sheffield had a unique custom; All the children, rich and poor alike, would have new cloths to wear on Whitsunday. Then all the churches and chapels would get together in their local parks in what ever district they were. The Boys Brigades, the Girl Guides Brigades, The Salvation Armies and all the spin-off groups of the churches would be included. To get to the parks the churches would organize parades which would be headed by a chosen May Queen for that year. The route would be planned in such a way that all the churches going to the district parks would be able to join the parade on route

A Whitsuntide Parade

where it would have swollen a hundred times or more.

All manner of transports were used to carry the May Queen, such as the local coal lorry, the brewery wagon, a horse and cart and there was always an abundance of lorries from the steel firms in Sheffield.

When they arrived at the park, the queens in their chosen mode of transport would be lined up at one end, making a backcloth for the whole scene. The church banners would be lined down either side. These would become the walls to the large outdoor church. The banners were about 5ft. square, sometimes bigger. They were all beautifully painted, usually depicting some biblical scene. Some scenes represented the group's own activity or cause, such as the Salvation Army, the Women's Voluntary Services, the Boys Brigade, the Brownies, the Scouts, etc. If you were chosen to help carry one of these banners, it was deemed as a great honour.

On this day the children would show off their new clothes and, for doing this, they would be given a few coppers by friends and neighbours. It was a bit like Christmas carolling, but instead of singing you would do a little twirl. It was this year that we nearly didn't get to show off any new clothes at all. This year had been very hard and money was scarce. Mum never let on, but she hadn't got the price of a little dress, let alone the undies that are supposed to go with it. However, God smiles in the darkest hours and he did just that for Mum. It was about two weeks before Easter and Mum was getting very desperate. No matter how poor you were, you were expected to at least put your child into something new.

It was Saturday afternoon and Dad was calling Mum to come upstairs, but Mum was reluctant to go to him knowing that he had just left his friends at the pub. After a little persuasion she did eventually go up to him. I heard her scream out his name. I dashed up stairs expecting the worst. On my way up she was saying to Dad "You've pinched it! Oh Archie, you shouldn't have done that." Then Dad was saying " For the last time Nanc, I've won it." With that, he pulled a piece of paper out of his pocket and was pointing to something in the newspaper. I was just staring down at the fifty, one pound notes spread out on the bed. It was more money than I had ever seen in my life. It was a small fortune in those days. As I looked up at Mum, she looked at me and said "He hasn't pinched it Nancy love, He's won it." She then put her arms around Dad's neck and kissed him.

That Whitsuntide was one of the best ever. Within two days, all of us had some thing new to wear, including Mum and Dad. Mum looked lovely in her new dress and Dad got a new shirt. I just wished that he would wear a coloured one for a change instead of always wearing white. It turned out to be an exceptional Whitsunday as we spent the whole day as a family. We went to the Whit-sings in the park. On the way back we called in on Gran and when she saw Dad, she said to him "I thought you'd died." I just thought it was an odd thing to say to someone who wasn't even poorly. At least, I didn't think he was, because we all went to the club that night. It had been a wonderful day.

It was near to my tenth birthday when I was told about my next operation. I was going to have my top lip reshaped. It still had a small tuck in it. Mr. Hynes was going to smooth this out and give me a cupids-bow. I must have looked at him funny, because he started laughing and then he said "Let me explain. Your top lip should have a dip in the middle of it, like all beautiful young ladies have, so that when you are older you will able to wear lipstick and make up." As he was saying these last words he was looking towards Mum. It sounded good to me. From now on I would look forward to the time when I could wear lipstick like all the lovely ladies in the books I had seen. Soon after this time I was put into a Christmas show at school so, instead of the operation being done at the beginning of December as planned, I was asked if I would like to do the show and then go into hospital for Christmas. I jumped at the chance. It was my first show and I would get to spend Christmas with my 'friends' the nurses. With the innocence of a child I didn't give my parents feelings a thought. It must have been devastating for them to learn that I wanted to spend Christmas in hospital instead of at home.

The play was to be the first I had ever done. Most children at my age would have appeared in some show or pantomime, be it at school, or church. I had never been chosen until then. I remember wanting to cry while the teacher was putting my make up on, but she kept telling me how good I was going to be and that I should speak out loud, and not to forget to smile.

I was feeling very important, but very nervous because I had to do the opening speech. As the curtains opened I was surprised to see only the first few rows, then towards the back only darkness. I searched frantically for Mum and Gran's friendly faces. I had been told that they had arrived and that I had to do my very best for them. I could hear myself saying the first few words, but it didn't sound like me saying them. It sounded like an echo. I was to soon realize that it was the microphones. My opening speech ended with a round of applause and the show was on.

Somewhere in the show I was a turtle. We had shells made out of cardboard on our backs and fronts and I, along with a line of others, had to fall to the ground and land on our backs so that our legs and arms were free to wave in the air. On a given signal we all fell down. I landed on my knees, first expecting to swing my legs round but the cardboard made the second movement impossible. So I just laid back and must have looked like a decapitated turtle, with everyone else's arms and legs going fifty to the dozen and only my arms taking part in the show. My legs were beginning to hurt so much I was longing for the end of the scene so that I could stand up while I could still feel them. When the end of the scene came we had to stand up and swim our way off stage. The signal came for us to get up but I could not move. The cardboard on my back kept my legs prisoner while the cardboard on my front would not allow me to bend up. Try as I might I just could not move. As one of the teachers came to my aid I was aware of the laughter coming from the audience. I'd hoped that they weren't laughing at me but I'm afraid they were. However, I did get a clap for the little bit of extra entertainment I had provided and it didn't stop me from appearing in future productions at the school.

It was getting very near Christmas now and still the letter hadn't come. I was hoping that they hadn't forgotten about me. When it did finally drop through the letter box it was very distinctive, being the only buff coloured envelope in amongst the white enveloped Christmas cards. I was to go into hospital on the 23rd December 1947.

We got up on the morning of this day. I remember Dad being at home when he should have been at work. He gave me some comics and told me I could read them while I was in the hospital. He kissed me then kissed Mum and then he was gone. My aunty came a few minutes later. She was going to baby sit while Mum and Mrs. Kerkhoff took me into hospital. She gave Mum a small parcel, whispered something in her ear and Mum put the parcel in my hospital bag.

We got off the bus at Fulwood church and started to walk towards the drive leading down to the hospital. It was very, very cold. The wind felt like sheer ice on my cheeks. Mrs. Kerkhoff had come with us to help carry the parcels and bags, at least that is what I was told. Now I am older, I think not. The drive was very icy and the three of us were trying to hold each other up. I was in the middle. As each of my elders did a little slip their grasp on my hand would tighten a little. It was fun trying to hold them up, until my right hand was vacant and poor Kerkhoff was on the floor. She had put her foot on a little puddle that was covered with ice. The ice gave way and down went Kerkhoff. As she got up she was covered in mud from the puddle and she had torn her stocking. Mum looked at her, they both looked at me and we all started laughing together. Now, when Kerkhoff starts to laugh, everybody starts to laugh and she laughs more. So now she is covered in mud, I have stomach ache with laughing and Mum has tears running down her face with laughing. Well at least it broke the icy silence that had been on the bus. We arrived at the hospital door and, as we opened it, a nurse was passing by. Kerkhoff just looked at her and said "Don't ask" and we set off with a little laugh this time. As we walked down the corridor it was like being in Wonderland. It was all trimmed up in silver and blue with large silver stars down the centre of the corridor to the very end. But there was no big Christmas tree.

We were taken into the office as usual and Mum had to answer much the same questions as usual. Then we were taken to the ward. We turned into the big double doors and there it was, the biggest Christmas tree I had ever seen in a room. It was something out of a story book and the lights were going on and off. To me it was as if it had been done by magic. My bed was half way down the ward. If I knelt on the bed I could just see over the window bottom, out onto the garden below. Before Mum left she gave me two parcels to put under the tree and Kerkhoff gave me one to give to the nurse in charge.

Mum and Kerkhoff stayed with me for a while. They were given a hot drink and one of the nurses put a plaster on Kerkhoff's knee and gave her a pair of stockings to go home in. When they went I took them to the door and waved them off. These days the nurses trusted me not to run off.

As I walked back down the corridor one of the nurses was walking towards me. She smiled and said "Would you like to look out into the garden?" I answered her question with a nod. She took my hand and we went through the ward with the French windows in it. She pointed to a line of trees at the bottom end of the garden and told me if I looked out after tea I would see all these trees lit up. I was taken back to my ward. I was allowed to stay up and better still, I didn't have to get undressed. Now this was something totally new. When I had been admitted before, I had to undress before Mum went home and she would take all my clothes with her. Not any more.

At lunchtime all the patients who were allowed out of bed sat around the big table in the middle of the ward. We were a motley crew of people; some with arms in slings, others had face bandages and some with feet sticking out of a plaster cast. Most were women and one or two children. Some of the people I was in with this time had been promised that they could go home for Christmas Day, so the atmosphere was very light and happy.

I helped to clear the dinner pots off the table then we were allowed to get the games out. These times were great social occasions where we would share chocolates, tell each other jokes and some of the nurses would be the butt of the jokes. But it was all in good part.

It went dark before tea time and I couldn't wait until after tea to see the lights. So I walked up the corridor to the ward with French windows. There were four ladies in the ward. When they saw me they said "You couldn't wait until tea time then?" I shook my head feeling a little bit shy. I looked through the glass. I could see the trees with the lights on, but the lights were on in the ward so the reflection dazzled the view. Then one of the ladies said "Wait a bit." She got off her bed, put the lights out and when I turned around, there they were. They shone out brightly from the darkness of the night. After tea I had a chance to see them again and I became friends with the four ladies.

On Christmas Eve there was a lot of activity going on in the hospital. The nurses were packing for the people who were going home for good, or just for the holiday period. All this activity seemed to be over by lunch time, so after lunch we cleared the table to start with the games and other activities. It was at this point that I was asked if I would like to be a Christmas fairy and go around on a trolley on Christmas Day giving out presents to people who had none. My answer was a quick "Yes please." Yards of gauze, which was usually used for dressings, were quickly gathered into a skirt, someone else cut out a bodice. The whole thing would be tied around my waist with a bandage. Two wings were made from gauze being stretched over some wire, and then the whole thing was covered in tinsel trimming and the crowning glory was made from wire, with some silver tape wound around it. To put the finishing touches to this work of art one of the nurses put a brooch in the middle of the crown and, oh, I was the best fairy for miles around.

That evening after supper we all had to be in bed a little earlier. No-one understood why until in the distance we heard the very faint sounds of carol singing. It was a sound I have remembered to this day. When the carol changed they were always a little nearer and, as they got nearer, the lights on the corridors and wards were going out. At last the singers got to our ward. The lights went out as they began to sing Once in Royal David's City. It was then we noticed the singers were the doctors, nurses and friends from the church. Each one was holding a lantern. The whole scene was like a fairy tale. The choir were dressed in their purple robes. There was a fairy, a Father Christmas and various other Christmassy costumes. The procession made its way down the ward to stand and sing another carol. The priest said something, we said a prayer and then the whole picture faded out of sight through the doors and the singing faded into the distance once more.

Christmas day dawned with much the same routine until after breakfast. We all had to sit by our beds. The doors at the end of the wards opened and there was Father Christmas and, whether you believe or not, the magic of seeing him never fades. Not even for a little girl who knows.

He came down the ward and now everyone was laughing at him saying "Ho, Ho, Ho." He gave out his presents then he was gone. Now it was my turn and the nurses brought my new fairy dress. They helped me to get dressed then they sat me on a trolley with loads of presents. There was also another little boy dressed in a pixie outfit. He had got very badly burned so he was from the burns part of the hospital. That is where we started our Christmas adventure. In every ward we went to we seemed to get more presents given to us than we were giving out; sweets, money, fruit and some toys. After that ride I was allowed to keep the dress on for the rest of the day and for two or three days after. I particularly remember wearing it on New Years Eve. My Mum asked me if I would be allowed to keep it. I said that I didn't know. She encouraged me to ask one of the nurses, who was really a bit of a tease. She said "No I'm sorry, but we need the gauze for the patients dressings." At that age you actually believe what a grown up is telling

The Christmas Fairy

you. I felt so disappointed I almost started to cry, until I saw her mischievous smile. Before Mum left that night I had taken the dress off and put it in a bag so that she could take it home with her. I wasn't taking any chances on someone changing their minds about it.

After supper I was told that I would be having my operation on the second of January. That was the first time I can remember being told the exact day when I would be going for an operation. Usually I would be woken up and then told "Today you are going to theatre." All of a sudden I felt grown up.

Later that evening, as on Christmas Eve, we were told to get into bed a little earlier than usual. All the grown ups had had the privilege of knowing why. Some minutes later I heard a bell ringing and someone saying something as they walked down the corridors and wards. In the background someone was singing hymns very, very softly. When the doors opened at the top of the ward the lights went out and, as on Christmas Eve, a little group of people came in carrying lanterns and stood at the far end of the ward. Someone started to say something about the old year. Then a boy and an old man came forward. The old man was holding the little boy's hand, He said a few words and, as the old man finished, he shook hands with the boy then disappeared into the gathering of people behind him. Though I didn't like him at first I felt quiet sad when he had disappeared. Then, with the boy leading them, they all left the ward.

I awoke the next morning to the sound of the breakfast trolley. It had gone past my bed and for a while I was in fear of having none, because I knew what that meant. However, they came back to me after finishing the rest of the ward. The nurse smiled at me saying "Happy New Year Nancy" then she kissed me. In the middle of breakfast someone said "It's snowing." By the time I had had breakfast and got dressed there was a thin layer of snow over the garden. It was a dark morning and the outside tree lights had been turned on. The scene for me was magical as I stood looking out of the French windows. The rest of the day was spent much the same as any pre-operation day with tests and questions by different people.

It was January 2nd 1948. When I woke to the usual sounds of the wards; the sound of washing basins being given out, the bed pans rattling on the trolleys and there was always someone calling for one in desperation with, finally, a big thank you when they got it. Every morning somewhere in amongst this rabble and turmoil the sister of the ward made her appearance. Usually she would busy herself giving orders to the nurses but today she came straight to my bed. "Happy New Year Nancy. You know what today is don't you?" I nodded in reply.

Instead of breakfast I was given an operation pack. I was taken for my bath then put back to bed, much to my surprise. Had they just forgot the enema? I cautioned an inquiry. I was relieved to learn later that it had been stopped. I didn't bother to ask why.

I was dressed in my oversized woolly socks and operational gown waiting for the pre-med to be given. The ward domestics were doing their usual chores. I was still hoping they would move my bed along with the others but they didn't, so putting the seal on what I already knew. The nurse arrived with the kidney shaped dish in her hand. She didn't have to tell me to roll over as I was already there. Then she sat talking to me about how I would feel after the operation. She said "You already know what you're having done, but when you wake up your lip will feel very sore and swollen. It will look very nasty for a while, but don't worry about it. It will get better." Now when I look back I sometimes wonder who she was trying to convince, herself or me?

As the nurse had predicted I did wake up with a sore lip and a swollen face. As I started to look around me I could see the screens, but they weren't screens this time. They were nice new curtains, curtains that could be pulled around each bed. I was looking at the patterns when a nurse came in saying "Oh, you're awake are you?" She disappeared behind the curtain again. When she came back the sister was with her and she was saying "Hello sleeping beauty. Are you feeling all right? No sickness?" As soon as she said that, I did feel sick. There was a lot of vomiting after operations in those days. I would have drifted in and out of sleep for most of the day after that.

When I did finally wake up to reality it was to the sound of breakfast being served and the usual chatter in the ward. Something, however, was different. The Christmas trimmings had gone and my lovely big Christmas tree had gone with them. I felt cheated. I wasn't given one more chance to look at them. If only someone had told me they wouldn't be here when I came round from the operation, I could have had a last look. However, there was still the snow to look at. When I was able to sit up I could just see over the window sill that was behind the nurses desk. For days after the operation my mouth, face and lips were very painful and swollen. I was back to being drip fed but after a few days, and much sooner than I had anticipated, I was allowed to have some very cool soup.

At last, the friendly face of Mr. Hynes came into the ward. He sat on a chair next to the bed. As he held my hand he said "I hope we're still friends." He went on to say "I know it hurts now, but in a few weeks when it gets better you will look a lot better, I promise. This has been a very big operation for you but it is the last one, though you will have to have a few more little ones. For now it is looking very good for you and, with your new shaped lip, you will be able to wear lipstick and make-up, but only when you are old enough or you'll get me shot. Do you hear?" Then he was gone again.

I recall it was one of the longest times spent in the hospital. Due to the nature of the operation I must have looked almost freakish, with my top lip swollen out of all proportion due to the soft tissue of the lips and my nose ballooned to twice its size. If I had been sent home I would have probably frightened everybody to death. It was while I was in hospital Mum told me that she was having another baby. This would be her seventh child. I was to get a baby brother or sister in April. Dad still didn't come to visit me as often as Mum and Grandma did. When a new visitor came it was a thing to remember, like the time when one of my school friend's mother came to see me. She was a nice lady and she spoke to Mum whenever they met at school. I remember her as one of the very few people I knew who had a car in those days. She brought me a blouse that fitted just under a pinafore dress. The blouse was white with a little lace collar and the dress was a lovely shade of green. I wore this dress long after it should have been made into dusters. That's what clothes were turned into when one had finished wearing them. Along with the outfit she gave me some jelly in a jar. It was Strawberry flavoured. At tea time I asked if I could have a dish to put my jelly in. By now I was eating more solid foods. I tipped the jelly into the dish. It didn't wobble like a jelly should. In fact it looked more like jam and, of cause, it was jam. Now no-one told me that jam could also be known as 'jelly'. I didn't want to look stupid so I ate the whole jar and vowed never to tell a soul what I had just done.

Soon after this I had the stitches on the outside of my lip removed.

The removal of sutures is painful at any time but when they are on the lip it is more so. There were no numbing injections then. I was told that I would have the inside stitches taken out in a few days time. I was relieved to hear this at the time. When the time came to have the other sutures removed I was petrified. In the middle of the morning a nurse came to tell me that I would be having the rest of the stitches out. I remember telling her that they didn't hurt me and I was all right. She could see I was scared to death so she called for the sister on the ward. When she came she couldn't understand why I was so frightened of such a little operation, after I had had so many. It turned out that someone had forgotten to tell me that the inside stitches would have to be removed by local anaesthetic. After this reassurance I was fine.

I left hospital four weeks after the operation but I wasn't allowed back to school for a long time after that. I was allowed to play out in the neighbouring streets and everyone who knew me just accepted me for who I was, but I always knew that any strangers would give me a hard time by staring a little too long or just eliminate me from their circle all together. When this happened I just took my cue and went home. I did start to wonder whether Mr. Hynes had been lying when he said I would be nice looking.

I went back to school about eight weeks into the New Year. I was still having speech therapy once a week, but now all the concentration was on my lips; learning how to use them and building up the muscle power in them. I soon got back into the routine of school again and there was the new baby to look forward to. Somehow I didn't seem interested. It was just another baby to me. Just after Easter my sister, Joyce, was born and she was beautiful, so tiny and immediately I was playing mother to her.

It was just after this that a nightmare started for me. I had gone to school on that Monday morning. I was playing in the school yard before the bell calling us to class was rung. It was at this moment I remembered I hadn't been to the toilet and begged to be excused. We had to go through the cloakroom to get to the toilets. As I walked in I was shocked to see an older boy standing there. He looked very surprised to see me. I knew he should not have been there. It was not his side of the school and he should have been in class. He just stood there looking at me. Now, I had seen him in the playground and knew he was a bully and the way he was looking at me now scared me. So I cancelled my trip to the toilet and went back to my class. All morning I could see those eyes. Even though he wasn't in my class I could see him. The dinner bell rang. All the school ate in one big hall and I knew I would see him there and, sure enough, there he was looking right at me. I was sitting down waiting for my dinner when the nightmare started.

A teacher, Miss Whaight, put her hand on my shoulder and said "Follow me Nancy." I got up and, as I did so, I had a feeling that something was wrong. I followed her across the yard in mother and duck fashion. I could see that we were heading towards the building that housed my class room, but instead of going to the class room we went into the cloak room. She said to me in a not too kindly voice.

"Which is your coat?" I pointed to it.

"Are you sure?"

"Yes Miss." I replied.

"Have you got anything in your pockets?" I shook my head.

"Are you sure?" I said "Yes Miss."

She then told me to put my hand into my pocket. I could feel money. Now I had a right to feel scared. There were two coins in it. I was almost too terrified to bring my hand out again because I knew the coins were not mine. Miss Whaight gave me one of her 'I'm waiting' looks. I withdrew my hand and there, in the middle of my palm, were two two-shilling pieces (40 pence). I could hardly believe my eyes. Miss Whaight was saying "Well, are they yours Nancy?" My eyes began to well with tears as I said "No."

"Then what are you doing with them?" I had no answer.

"I am afraid we will have to go and see Miss Elliott."

We went back across the playground at a much quicker pace than we had come. I was hoping that we wouldn't go through the dining room to get to her office but we did. I felt a thousand eyes were looking at me as a we wended our way through the diners.

A quick knock on the door and we were in that awful room with the butterflies. I had to stand in humiliation while Miss Whaight told her what she knew. Miss Elliott turned to me and said "Is this true Nancy?" I could only nod my head. I could see the big boy in my mind staring at me daring me to tell on him. Miss Elliott was now saying:

"How did the money come to be in your pocket?"

"I don't know Miss."

"Are you sure Nancy? It is better to tell the truth in an instant than to live a lie for the rest of your life. Do you hear me?" By this time I was in tears. I was telling the truth as far as I knew it, or was I? But I could not say anything for fear of what he would do to me.

Before I left for home that night I was given a sealed letter with strict instructions to hand it to one of my parents and no-one else. The letter burned in my pocket. I knew only too well what was in it. I got off the tram at the top of our road, but instead of going straight home I walked past my road to where I knew there was a waste bin. I looked at the letter then I tore it up and put it into the bin.

I recall Mum asking me if I was all right that night. She made a comment on how quiet I was. The next morning my class teacher asked me if I had got anything to tell her. I said "No". "Have you got a letter from home?" Again the answer was "No".

Nothing else was said for a few days until one day I went home from school. My mother was waiting for me. She was fuming. She was holding a letter and she was shaking with temper.

"What have you been doing? Where is the letter from school?"

"I Haven't got it. I threw it away"

"They are saying you stole some money. Did you?"

"No. If I tell you what happened you won't tell anyone will you Mum?" By this time I was close to tears. I told her about the boy, how the teacher made me find the money in my own pocket and how I couldn't tell on the boy because he would get me. I thanked God that she knew her own daughter. The next morning Mum took me to school. I went to my class as usual and Mum went to see Miss Elliott. I never did find out what Mum had said to the headteacher that day. I can't remember ever seeing that boy again and all the teachers were nice to me again. Yes, I liked being at Maud Maxfield School for the deaf.

CHAPTER 4

MAKING CHANGES

Life was beginning to get into a familiar pattern at home; getting up for school, a rushed breakfast, help to dress the little ones. Mum was looking very pregnant now and she was always tired, but I never saw her idle. She was always washing some clothes, usually dirty nappies or ironing Dad's shirt so he could go out in it that night. She never complained, but the phrase "Oh Nancy love...." was often on her lips.

In the east end of Sheffield life was very hard and tough for young and old, both men and women. The steel workers were as hard as the steel they worked with, but inside their homes the wives and families could find their soft spots. They would never ever be caught washing the dishes or doing housework of any kind. They regarded that as women's work. The bringing up of children was left to the mother, but the father always had the last word and when dad spoke it was usually the final word to any argument or choice.

A week or so after the money problem I was given another letter to take home. It was about a trip to London. If I could go I would have to pay a deposit now and the rest later. Mum read the letter and I could tell by her face what the answer was going to be. She said "Sorry love." I pleaded with her at length:
" It's only five shillings (20 pence) deposit."
"And two pounds to pay at the end of it." Came the reply.
"And what about spending money? Where will that come from?"
"Oh go on Mum. I'm sure Gran will give me something to go with."
"No Nancy. If I do it for you I've got to do it for the others and I can't afford it." I almost said "They can't go" but I didn't. I needed her on

my side so I thought I'd try later on. I did try later but to no avail, so I took the little tear off slip at the bottom of the letter back with the 'yes' box crossed off. When the day for the trip to London arrived those that were not going to London were told that a trip to Matlock Bath had been arranged. We were told to take sandwiches and the drink would be provided. There were two coaches at the school gates. The one in front was for London. As we arrived at the gate this coach was almost full and the parents were shouting through the windows to the children inside, telling them to be good and not to get into trouble.

When this bus pulled away, we were all told to wave good bye. We all did as we were told, but not with any enthusiasm because ninety percent of us wanted to go to London. I can remember very little about my first day in Matlock bath, except that it had a strange name and that we had to write about it when we got back to school on Monday. Apparently the Victorians were very fond of spa baths.

I was at Maud Maxfield school for almost two years. I was very happy there. I felt wanted, no, 'needed'. I felt needed because I was the one who showed the visitors around our class and told them what we did in our lessons. I was the one with the speaking parts in the two pantomimes and a play. Yes, I felt needed. But I was set to leave at the end of 1948.

I wasn't aware of it at the time, but there was a debate going on between the education department and my parents as to which school I should go to next. I could go back into main stream schooling. Having very little knowledge left on how a 'normal' school is run, I had had very little academic schooling over the previous two years and there was the other element; Children were very honest and therefore could be very cruel. So weighing all the pros and cons of the problems I could be faced with, they agreed it would be better if I went to an open air school.

There were two open air schools in Sheffield. One was Whitely Woods and the other was Bents Green. They were both in the Ringinglow district. These schools were for children with health problems and there may have been a percentage of one with my problem.

It was decided that I would go to Bents Green. This was to be a stepping stone back into mainstream schooling. It was while I was at this school that I decided to change my name. It was here I would go down in history as one of the few students who never took the 'eleven plus' exam. It was here I got caned followed by an apology.

Mum received a letter from Bents Green inviting her to come and have a look around. She was told to bring me with her. Ringinglow was one of Sheffield's much better areas. It felt like I was going on a day trip because the journey took that long. When we got of the tram, we had to walk about half a mile up a beautiful tree lined road. We passed some very big houses and some had cars on the drive ways. As we approached a small sign Mum said" I think that's it Nancy." We turned into what looked like a private house. Mum stopped and wondered if there was another way in, but there didn't appear to be, so we tentatively made our way up the drive.

As we walked up the drive we could see a large house. This was covered in ivy from the ground to the guttering. It had been cut back around the windows. I remembered Mum saying "Oh Nancy. I'm sure this is not it. It can't be." As we approached the large front door we could see a small notice at the side. It was telling us to go to the side door so we went around the end of the building. By the time we had got there someone had opened it and was saying "hello." We had obviously been watched. The lady invited us to follow her through the house. She was asking me if I would be a resident or a day student. Mum answered that I would be a daily.

We had to walk through the house, out of the back door, across the playground and then up the side of another building that looked as old as house itself. The window that we passed on the side of this building was to be used a lot during the time I was here, but now we were being shown into an office at the end of the path.

Miss Wostenholm, the headteacher, wasn't in when we arrived, so we were told to take a seat while the lady went for her. While we were sat there we had a chance to look out of the windows at the lovely view over the valley. The other window looked out onto one of the four square class rooms that were set slightly back one from the other, so that when you went on the paths past the class rooms it was like a rick rack pattern.

After a few minutes the door opened and Miss Wostenholm came in, with a gust of wind helping her to come in a bit quicker. She remarked on the wind that was getting up and then said "You must be Mrs. Mallender and you must be Nancy. It's nice to meet you at last." We shook hands and then she told us about the school.

There were seven class rooms. Five of them were the square type we could see from the office. The others were housed in a brick terrapin building. We were told that breakfast was served to every pupil each morning, residents and none residents alike. After lunch every one of the pupils had a lie down. The first dinner sitting would have an hour and a half and second would have an hour. Being on the first sitting was good at first, but I began to favour the second, especially in the summer. Miss Wostenholm went on to say that before leaving for home, all the children were given a small tea, such as bread and butter or scones along with tea, milk or hot chocolate. No choice, you just got what was given to you on the day. To me this school sounded just as good as Maud Maxfield, if not better. After our talk we were shown to the class room that I would be in.

The teachers name was Miss Jubb. I don't remember much about her, except that she was always smiling and nice to me. I think the reasons that I don't remember any of the teachers precisely are firstly that I wasn't at any one school long enough, and secondly that at this school, we had different teachers for different lessons. As we left we passed the window at the side of the office. I was told that this was from where I would collect a blanket every day after dinner and return it after the rest period. Last of all we were shown the correct way in and out. It was a path adjacent to the main drive. It was hidden from view by a tall hedge that divided them.

Before we parted, Miss Wostenholm reminded me that I should be in Leopold Street at nine o'clock prompt on Monday morning, where I would catch the special bus. The next bit was aimed more at my mother than me; "If you miss the bus you will have to go into the school clinic on Leopold Street and ask for some tokens to be used on public transport to school." We shook hands again and she was gone.

On Monday morning just before nine, Mum and I were stood in a queue waiting for the special bus to arrive. I'm sure to this day we were stood in the coldest street on earth. It was freezing and would stay so for a few more weeks yet. When the bus came Mum was told to pick me up at four in the afternoon.

When we arrived at the school gates, we were told to form two lines. We were then marched up the path at the side of the drive. Still dressed in our coats, we were shown into a dining room where we were given a breakfast of warm porridge and a mug of hot milk. After breakfast I was told to wait in my seat for a teacher. Now this was a bit unnerving, to be told to wait in an empty room that, until a moment ago, was filled with about fifty laughing, chattering children. There were two other children in with me, but my feelings were still on edge because I hadn't been told why I had wait there.

It felt like a lifetime, but it was only a few minutes before a teacher came into the room and told us to gather around her. She gave each of us a small toilet bag. In it was a toothbrush and paste, some soap, a flannel and a comb. The bag had a number on it. Mine was thirty seven. The teacher explained that this would be our number from now on. It would be on my coat peg and on my blanket after dinner and it would be on the little cot bed that would be given to me in the class room.

So, holding our little toilet bags we were taken to the wash room. Here we had to wash our hands and clean our teeth. We were taken from here to see the nurse where we were stripped, all but for our pants. This didn't bother me, but the girl, Barbara who I later befriended, started to cry saying she didn't like it. It turned out to be a routine medical.

We arrived at our classes well into the morning lessons. Barbara and I were left with Miss Jubb and the boy that was with us was taken to another class. I liked my new teacher from the moment I saw her. Lunchtime came around surprisingly quickly that day. When the bell rang there was no mad dash for the door. Instead all the people in the class started to stack the chairs in a corner of the room and the tables were stacked one on top of the other down one side. Then everyone formed a queue at the back of the class while Miss Jubb shouted out the numbers on the sides of the beds. The beds were basically a wooden frame with two sets of legs that folded in underneath for stacking purposes. A canvas was stretched lengthways over the frame and secured with a lace underneath. At first I liked being on the earlier dinner so I could have a long rest, but the novelty of this soon wore off, especially in summer when the others were out playing and you were in bed. At first I was given an old brown blanket that had a hole in it right where I would find my foot going through it, if I wasn't very careful. I would have a job getting my foot back in before the teacher saw me and whispered very loudly "Nancy, stop wriggling." It wasn't long before I got into the swing of things and a new routine of school, home, work and bed were established.

By this time I had had about fourteen operations and the last one was beginning to fade into a distant memory, except for the fact that I could see a difference in the shape of my top lip. I was beginning to think about what I would look like in make-up. I couldn't try Mums because Dad never let her wear it and there was another thought; Would he let me wear it?

It was only a couple of weeks after I had started this new school that I was left to find my own way to Leopold Street, in the centre of Sheffield. Now, while Mum was taking me to the bus she made sure that we were never late, because if we had missed the bus she knew that she would have had to take me all the way herself and she could neither afford the time or the money for the fare for the transport. So she made sure the situation didn't arise. When I was on my own it didn't seem to matter that I might miss the bus, after having run to the corner shop for a loaf or some sugar that we might need before we could have breakfast.

The first time I did miss the bus it was raining heavily and I was scared that the public transport bus was going a totally different way to the special bus. A woman on the bus asked me if I was all right. I told her about being late and that I thought the bus was going the wrong way. She was very reassuring. She told me to get off the stop after her. She assured me that I would recognize where I was once I was off the bus.

I got to school wet through and very late. I can't remember being scolded for it, but I remember the drink of hot milk I was told to drink and to "be quick."

One day when I arrived home from school Mum said to me "I've got a letter here for you. Shall I read it to you?" I said "No. I'll read it." I quite liked reading my own letters now. It was from the hospital saying that Mr. Hynes wanted me to go to the Grand Hotel in Sheffield. He was holding a seminar there and would like all his friends to see how well I was doing. Well, neither of us knew what a seminar was. However, when they said we would be in invited to stay for tea, now that bit appealed to both of us. We were to reply as soon as possible so that a date could be arranged.

It was a month later that we were being shown where the Sheffield's Grand Hotel reception was. I was wearing some new shoes and my Whitsuntide clothes. For the first time I felt I was grown up and rather

The Grand Hotel, Leopold Street. Now replaced by the Fountain Precinct

nervous, By the look of Mum she was feeling the same way. While we were waiting for someone to show us where the meeting was, the receptionist told us that we had just missed the singer Paul Robeson. He was appearing at the City Hall that night and he had just left for a rehearsal.

A porter came up to us, gave a little bow and asked if we would come this way please. We followed him up a beautiful staircase and along a corridor where he knocked on one of the doors. The door was opened, the young porter stepped aside and we were admitted. I can't remember a thing about the room. All I saw was two lines of faces, mostly male, and in front of them all, sat on one of the two chairs, was Mr. Hynes. When he saw us he got up, shook hands with Mum and said he was very pleased to see me again. He offered me the chair next to him and then spoke to the two rows of people, who turned out to be future surgeons.

He didn't sit down but started to say that I was one of his successes and that without the hard work from both of them, meaning Mum and myself; he could not have had the success he enjoyed today. He explained about the reshaped nose, about the new throat and about all the hard work it took to make dormant muscles work at the back of the throat. He continued that she still had the cleft palate and said "Unfortunately there wasn't enough skin tissue left on the roof of the mouth to pull it together. So Nancy wears a special palate with four teeth on it. But now we come to the last bit. Her last operation was to give shape to the top lip and I think that is going to be a success too." He was looking at me when he said:

"What do you think?" I just nodded my head in answer.

"Now, I'm just going to ask Nancy to do something for me."

He came and knelt down at the side of my chair and asked me in a very low voice if I would read the rhyme that was on the paper. I said "Yes" to the first part and then he said "Will you read it again without your dentures in?" I wasn't quite sure about the last request but I reluctantly said "Yes." I read the rhyme with ease then a dish was put in front of me. This was to put the teeth into. It was then covered with a cloth and I got a reassuring nod from Mr. Hynes.

I really didn't want to do this because I knew very well what would happen. I started to speak, but all that came out of my mouth was open, indistinguishable noises. After the first line I stopped. Very quickly my teeth were given back to me and just as quick Mr. Hynes was giving me a big hug and saying "Good girl." I could hear the people in the rows clapping and then someone said tea is served. We were shown into a smaller room where the tables and chairs were set. Mum and I were told to help ourselves to anything we wanted.

Now dining out was something that neither Mum nor I were used to doing. It just wasn't done where we came from and there weren't that many restaurants around. So to see all this fare on the table was new to us and the size of the sandwiches was a shock. Mum said something about our postage stamps being bigger than these, but the cups for the tea were beautiful china and the little plates were delicate like the little cakes and sandwiches. The size of the sandwiches was a talking point for Mum for a long time to come.

Bents Green school is primarily for children with long-term illnesses and special needs, mine being a helping hand to get back into main steam schooling. The school has a very interesting history to it to say the least: Before 1774 there was some sort of dwelling on the place where the main house is sited today. Amongst the lands allotted to Lord John Murray of Banner Cross under the Ecclesall Enclosure Act, was Plot No. 129 on the High Moors plan. Lord John Murray conceived the idea of providing a public hostelry for the convenience of man and beast on this then lonely part of Ringinglow Moors. It was to be named the 'Sun'. On one part of the building is the date 1774 and on another part is the coat of arms of Lord John Murray, now to be seen at the east end of the building.

Some time after the place was opened as an inn, an altercation is said to have taken place between the landlord and an inebriated customer, ending in the tragedy depicted in Mrs. Hofland's romance of "The House on the Moors."

It was on July 13th, 1791 that the commissioners met at the Sun when commencing the proceedings leading to the enclosure of the commons of upper and nether Hallam. The following official notice published at the time in the 'Sheffield Register' confirmed the date as being June 22nd, 1791. The meeting was attended by Arthur Elliott, Joseph Outram and B. Chambers.

It was said that an angry crowd gathered around the approach to the Sun when the business of perambulation was about to proceed. The crowd followed on the heels of the commissioners as they went their way inspecting the property. The multitude became more menacing as the work proceeded, this being emphasized by the fact that the commissioners were afraid to pursue their labours for the time being. They did not continue until the military arrived for their protection.

It would appear that the house as a hostelry did not survive the tragedy described by Mrs. Hofland, as afterwards it ceased to be a licensed house.

Lord John Murray, the owner, died in 1787. His legal representative, the Duke of Athol, sold the house and grounds in 1814 to a Mr. Joseph Bishop, a land agent and surveyor. He then sold it to Mr. Albert Smith, the clerk to the Sheffield Justices, in 1829. The latter making extensive alterations to the property. Mr. Blakelock Smith, who subsequently became the owner of the estate, also made extensive alterations converting them into the present substantial and handsome mansion.

Bents Green lodge has in later years been the residence of Mr. H. K. Stevenson, late Member of Parliament for the Park division of Sheffield. Later it was owned and occupied by Mr. J. M. Allen and is now the property of the Sheffield Education Department.

Bents Green School was run more or less like any other when it came to maths, reading and writing, but the sports activities were very much in evidence. We used to have long walks in summer and winter and only when it rained were the walks cancelled. We did a lot of physical exercises and sports. This I loved after being told at my first school that I could not do these activities and here I was being good at them. When I was picked out to play in the rounders team it was like being picked for the Olympics.

I learned to swim in Millhouses Park Lido when I was about eight years old. By the nature of the deaf school, they never took any pupils swimming because of the fear of infections in the ears. However, in the Lido I got the chance to show how good a swimmer I was and I was pretty good at it too. I was entered for my first swimming race in the school. Parents were invited to cheer us on and as our race got started I was soon in front. We were halfway across the baths when I heard someone shouting "Turn." I turned, swimming now against the others only to find out that the command was for another race taking part in the other half of the baths. I did get a book for my pains though.

It was while I was here that I discovered my love of sewing, but only through a teacher who said I couldn't sew. I have a stubborn streak in me, born from my father and whenever anyone says I can't, I will do my best to prove them wrong and in this case I did just that. Miss Ryan was the sewing teacher, but she had her favourites and I was not one of them. No matter what sewing work I did, it was never right and I had to undo the lot and start again. After a few weeks of going into her class I was becoming very disillusioned about ever pleasing her, until one day she was off ill, and the sewing she had told me to undo the week before was still only half undone. Before the class started, the new teacher wanted to see what work we had done so far. Very tentatively I gave her mine and, much to my surprise, she praised it saying "Carry on like that and you'll soon have it done Nancy." So from that day I was a little bit naughty, but it was to work most of the time. Whenever Miss Ryan was disappointed with my work and I was told to go and undo it, I would undo a little bit then leave the rest. My grandmother had a saying "You can't please people all the time, but sometimes you can pacify them." This was one of those times.

A song that came out about this time was to give me some grief. Whenever I heard it on the radio I would want to turn it off. If anyone was singing it I would try to move out of ear shot. It was because of this song that I changed my name, at the age of fourteen. The song was 'Nancy' by Frank Sinatra. The most prominent line in the song was 'Nancy with the laughing face' which, in my innocence, I totally misinterpreted and so did most of my peers and so called friends. It seemed that they would be singing it whenever I was near or the ones that were not singing would just look at me and their thoughts were being transferred. I did learn to live with it though. I was very mature in these situations and ignored the instant provocation, but I would be seething inside.

I asked the teacher if I could change my name to Anne, but she said "No you can't." I asked Mum if I could change it. She asked "Why?" I just said that Annie was my real name so why couldn't I be named as Anne or even Annie if it had to be, but I hated Annie. It sounded old fashioned, but at this moment in time anything was better than Nancy. For a long time I pestered Mum to let me do it, but only when I told her the absolute reason for the need to change my name did we come to a compromise. I would have to wait until I changed schools again, which was not until the end of the year and then if I still felt the same about it Mum would help me. She warned me that it would not be easy. Lots of

people would still call me Nancy and my dad would definitely not stop calling me Nanc. So what did I want to be called?
"Anne" was my answer.

Soon after starting Bents Green School I got a new red blanket. It was very thick and fluffy. I remember it was heavy too. A boy who was in another class offered to carry it for me and I took up the offer, but before we got to the class I was in I was called aside by a teacher and asked where was my blanket. I turned to say "He was carrying it for me" only 'he' wasn't there. I turned back again to the teacher. Again she put the question to me. I told her about the boy. She asked me what class he was in and I said I didn't know. I was told in not too light a term never let any one carry my things again. She sent me to my own class to explain to my own teacher the absence of my blanket. She told me to get my coat off the peg and put that over me until such times as I found it again. I started to cry thinking that I had had such a nice blanket and somebody had taken it.

As we got on the bus for home that night 'the boy' tapped me on the shoulder and told me that he couldn't find me to give me the blanket back, so he took it to the window. I thanked him, but the feeling of relief and joy at the thought of getting it back was tremendous.

I was eleven years old and, unknown to me, there was a discussion going on about whether or not I should take the compulsory 'Eleven Plus' exams, which every child had to do at the end of every academic school year. It was considered that I had not had enough normal education and so it would be futile to put me to this test, so the decision was taken not to let me sit the Eleven Plus. At the time I was among only a few hundred children who were exempt from this test.

Being at this school was not a particularly happy time nor was it a sad time. It was just a way of being eased into a normal school and that is exactly what it did. I began to stand up for myself and not to go running off to the teachers with my problems. I was reaching the age of self awareness. I was getting a dress sense and didn't very much like what I had to wear. Because we were poor we couldn't afford the better things in life. Mum would say "It's not what goes on your back, It's what goes into your stomach that keeps you going. If you haven't got good food you can't work and if you can't work there's no money."

I was nearly fourteen when I almost got myself killed. I was riding my brothers bicycle. It was one of my pleasures. I had to take it while he was out and go for a ride. Once or twice he would catch me and then the inevitable row would ensue, with Mum refereeing and finally parting us by giving us some job or other as a penance. I was riding down a steep hill and at the bottom was a corner that was usually very easy to negotiate, unless an irate brother was after you. I got up speed that a racer would have been proud of, spun around the corner only to be met by a slow moving car. I came off the bike, but got up and ran away. It was a long time before I dared to go home, but when I did I knew about it. Not only had the driver told my Dad about the crash, but my brother capped it by saying that I had taken the bicycle without him knowing about it.

I was feeling pretty bruised and knocked about a bit by now. As I went in the back door my Dad was waiting for me. He hit me across the head, spun me around and sent me straight upstairs to bed. I didn't know which part of me hurt the most; my leg was bleeding still through the little handkerchief I had tied to it and my side was grazed and bruised. I heard Dad saying to Mum "Leave her alone. She deserves to suffer." Later that night Mum did bring me a slice of bread and a drink, with instruction not to let any one know about it.

A few days earlier I had had a letter to go to Fulwood Annex for some new dentures. Mum just said "By the state of you they'll find you a bed and keep you." I had a bandage on my leg and, on closer examination, I had cut my hand when I fell off the bike, so now I had a bandage on my hand as well, plus the countless bruises.

As predicted, Mr. Raynor the dentist commented on me looking like a wounded soldier and I could only stand and cringe while Mum told him the whole sordid story. Mr. Raynor just said "Well, let's see what we can do towards getting you some new teeth and next time, do be careful because we have got used to having you around." I told Mr. Raynor that I intended to change my name after Christmas, because then I would be going to a new school. I don't think I had convinced him, but he just said light-heartedly "What's brought this on?" I didn't tell him the whole story. I just said I liked Anne better and that it was part of my own name. This seemed to satisfy him, but it didn't stop him checking the rumour with Mum: "I hear Nancy is changing her name when she goes to the new school." Mum replied "Yes. It's some silly idea she's got into her head, but if that's what she wants. I've told her it won't be that easy to do."

I got my new teeth just before Christmas and I had already started to change my name. We had to go to a pre-school meeting at Woodbourne Road School. Mum told them that I wished to be known as Anne from now on and that the papers coming from Bents Green would name me as Nancy. They were to be the last legal documents with the name Nancy on them.

After the New Year was safely on its way, the time had come to start my new school. I had been getting everyone around me used to calling me Anne. If my brothers and sisters got it right I would give them a treat from the biscuit tin, or a sweet if I had one, but the latter was still very rare because most of them were still on rationing. I had been beavering away like this since Christmas, so now at least I had the younger half of the family calling me Anne.

I hated the thought of going to school with Mum that first morning. I was fourteen and what would it look like. So I made arrangements to go a few minutes earlier with a friend who lived a few streets away from me, after which I would meet Mum there and go to the headteacher's study with her. Though it was my last school I don't remember one teacher's name, not even the head of school. I think all I wanted was for it to be over and done with as soon as possible. There were one or two memorable incidents while I was there. The friends I made couldn't understand why I had to change school in my final year. I just said that I had to and I wasn't sure why and left it at that. I had been at the school about three months when I was called to the head masters study. He wanted to remind me that there were five school days in the week and not four as I seemed to think. He wanted to know why I didn't seem to like Fridays at school. I told him that Mum needed me at home to look after the babies. He turned around from looking into a drawer, leaned over the desk and said, "Well Anne, she will just have to tell someone else to look after the babies won't she?" I was hoping he wasn't expecting me to tell her that. It would have been like signing my own death warrant. He started to write a note while I stood there in silence. He reached into a drawer took out an envelope ran his tongue across the top of it and said "Give this to your Mum, now go back to your class."

After this incident it was all right for a couple of weeks then Mum got the idea to go shopping in my dinner break. I had to rush home, she would be waiting at the door, I would have to get my own dinner more often than not then, just at the last moment, Mum would come back to let me go to school. I was getting fed up with always having to run back to school and often in the mornings I would be late. So a few weeks after my first encounter with the head I was waiting at his door again. There were four others waiting with me. When the door opened all five of us were marched into the room, which was a surprise to all of us. We were told to put our hands behind our backs and stand straight. He asked us if we knew why we were there. I had a good idea but said nothing. He stood behind his desk and picked up a cane. Now my heart was really beating. I had had the cane only once before, by Mr. Vardy at Bents Green School. It was said that I had been insubordinate to the nurse.

I had only been at Bents Green for a short time and the teachers weren't used to the pupils communicating on an adult level. I had been with adults more than the average child, so I spoke to them on that level. On the morning in question I was in the nurses room and she was looking through the children's hair. I can only think that it was my comments that got me into trouble while she was looking through my hair. From what I can recall I said something like "It's not always the clean jobs you do is it nurse?" and went on to comment "I don't know how you do it." She must have taken it in the wrong context, because after the caning I had to go and apologize to her and, while we were talking, I think she realised I had no intention of being rude to her, but that still didn't cure my stinging hand. Here I was in line for another, if only I could be certain why.

The head teacher asked us once again if we knew why we were there. This time one of the boys answered "Is it for being late sir?" "Yes it is." came the reply and what excuse have you for being late. I heard him concocting his reply. The cane moved to the next boy without being used. I was frantically trying to think of a good excuse but nothing was forthcoming. The cane was jabbed in my chest "And you?"
I was still fumbling for an answer, but all I could say in a very feeble voice was "I have no excuse Sir." The cane moved to the next chest until it reached the end of the line. Then once more I was jabbed in the chest. "You! Step forward. You are the only one here that has told the truth. There is no excuse for being late is there?" Then with one accord we all said "No." I was told to leave the room and not to let it happen again. I was amazed that for telling the truth I hadn't got caned. I

Fellow classmates at Bents Green School. Myself far right, front row aged 12

Myself aged 13

couldn't believe it.

I was Fourteen and a half when my parents took me to a dance at the working mens club. My parents never danced but they thought I might like to learn. The first night we went I don't think I had one dance but I enjoyed watching the others. Mum and Dad used to take me out every now and then as I kind of treat for looking after the little ones. I had been looking after them since I was ten years old and my treat was either a trip to the pictures or, more often, to a club where dad would play snooker and we would have to watch or if there was a good 'turn' on at the club we would go there. We started to go to the dances a bit more often than going any where else, so I learned to dance. A man who must have been as old as my father was my first teacher. It wasn't a fancy dancing class for me, it was this or nothing. So I learned to dance at the Radical Working Mens club in Attercliffe.

I was coming up to my fifteenth birthday when I had to go back into hospital for a minor operation. It was to remove a bit of bone from the roof of my mouth that was obstructing the proper fit of my dentures. While I was in the hospital I was asked if I would consider having the remaining top teeth removed. I think there were six or eight left. I didn't fancy having no top teeth and especially so near to Christmas so I said "No" but now the seed had been planted in my head. I started to look at my smile with the four little denture teeth at the front then the change of colour and shape of my own. I was beginning to not like what I saw. So when I went back for a check up on the operation, I discussed the possibilities of me having my teeth removed. I was told it would allow a much better fit for a denture palate and Mr. Raynor assured me that I would have no problem at all with them. However, if Mr. Raynor had told me that the world would fall on my head and that I wouldn't die, I'd believe him. He was that kind of man. You trusted him. He assured me that I would have to see Mr. Hynes, but that would not be until after Christmas now. I was very relieved to hear that last remark. I left Woodbourne Road School with no regrets. I wasn't leaving any bonded friendships behind. The two friends that I had made went with me to the club dance every week.

It was the December 27th 1952, less than a week after leaving school, that I started work as an assistant to a cook in Woodhouse's furniture stores in Sheffield. I liked the work very much, but I didn't know what was in store for me and Mrs. Turner, the cook.

This was my first grown up New Year. Mum and Dad were still having to take me into the club but they would leave me and my friends in the dance hall while they went into the snooker room. Dad would come back and top up our drinks and everything seemed fine. I had the company of boys who would dance with me, and some- times my friends would have to sit out. I got to be a good dancer, but then things started to change. I was earning a wage now, so I had to buy my own drinks. Dad would just bring me to the club, buy the first round. He would stand at the bar, drink his pint and then leave, with instructions that I had to leave the club at ten o'clock sharp.

I began to notice that the boys were there when me and my friends arrived with my father. They would have the first dance and maybe the second, but for the rest of the night that would be it. My girl friends were danced off their feet, while I had to rely on someone else to ask me, usually an older man who would be a friend of my father's. This went on for a few weeks before the reality of it sunk in. They danced with me whilst Dad bought the drinks.

It was a Tuesday night, the night of the dance. We arrived at the club door and I asked Dad not to come in with us. I was with my two friends. He said "If that's what you want OK, but I will have to sign you in." He signed us all in then went back home. Being only fifteen I wasn't allowed to buy drinks at the bar, so I asked one of Dad's friends to get them for me. I walked into the dance hall with the three orange juices. The friends that were already there were waiting expectantly. When Dad didn't follow me in they asked where he was. I told them they could stop sponging off my Father from now on. In my wildest dreams I didn't expect the reply I got from one of them. He said "Don't kid yourself. Your father asked us to dance with you. He asked us to give you a good time." I was flattened. The so called friends left and I was left with my two girl friends who could see how gutted I was. We didn't do much dancing that night, but just talked. By the end of the night I was convinced that I was going to show my Father I could make it without his help. I know he was only trying to help, but it didn't lessen the taste of the bitter pill I had just swallowed.

For the rest of the week Mum kept asking if every thing was all right. I just said "Yes" and left it at that. I didn't go to the dance for two weeks. My friends and I would go to the pictures and they would tell me what had happened at the dance. I really did miss it, but my ego had been deflated. I was resigning myself to another Tuesday night in, listening to the radio. Mum and Dad had gone out and I was baby sitting again. I washed my hair and put it up in rollers. They were all the rage then, these big rollers for longer hair. Mum and Dad then came back and I thought that they had forgotten something. I had just finished putting the rollers in and was sat trying to dry my hair in front of the fire. Hair dryers were a luxury then. Dad said to me "Get ready. You're going dancing." I reminded him that I'd just washed my hair and, besides, I was not bothered any more. He persisted and said "With or without rollers you're going to the club" and when Dad spoke like that you didn't disagree.

I was protesting all the way, saying that I wouldn't go in if 'they' were there. Dad never said a word. He was a tall man and his long legs strode out while I had to do a little trot to keep up with him. My hair was still a little damp when we got to the club. He took me straight into the dance to where my two girl friends were sitting. He just said to me "Are you all right now?" I just nodded my head then he said, with a little smile "Do you mind if I buy your friends a drink?" I said "No" and I knew then that was as near to an apology my Dad was going to give. He was never a man for apologies.

CHAPTER 5

FLASHING AND FINISHING

I began to feel so inadequate. I went very quiet and I built my own Wendy house again. I was fine while I was at work, but when I got home I was very different. I would do the necessary jobs around the house such as clearing the tea table, washing the dishes and so on. Wednesday was always wash day, so I had to scrub the kitchen floor. I didn't mind this because it usually took up most of the night. However, on other nights I would get it done then get the evening paper which was full spread. I would then sit in an easy chair that fitted slightly under a shelf and there I would make my own space until my parents went out and left me in charge of the younger ones, or it was time to get them to bed.

I know Mum tried to coax me out of this mood many times. It was about this time that she bought me my first real grown up dress. It was blue glazed cotton, fitted under the bust to the waist, then the skirt went out into a wide 'A' line. It made me feel like a queen. I would walk around with my hands in the two side pockets. I felt so grown up in it. I had started to wear make up and it made me look a lot older than my fifteen years. I was tall, had long dark hair and, when Dad wasn't around, I wore earrings. I could, and did, pass for eighteen, especially when I wanted to see an adult film. I still went to the dance, but now I felt that I was complying to an order and if I didn't go I would have to explain why.

I had seen Mr. Hynes and was now waiting to go into hospital to have my top teeth removed. I was still very nervous of the prospects of having no teeth for a few weeks. Prior to going into hospital I had to see Mr. Raynor. I thought it was just a routine check, or just checking to see if I had changed my mind, but when I arrived at Fulwood Annex I was pleasantly surprised to see Mr. Hynes there as well. They started to explain to me that I might not have to go without teeth. After I have the teeth out they were going to try something new. I was to have a new and temporary palate made before I have the operation. This would be made of a softer material and would see me through the first few weeks after having the operation. So I spent the next three or four weeks going back and forth to Fulwood Annex, a journey Mum and I had done many times over the years together, but now I was on my own. At the last fitting for the teeth I was told that a bed had been booked for me on the following Monday morning.

I arrived at the hospital early Monday morning and I was shown into a small side room. What was to follow next would sound better in a fiction novel and it would have to be a comedy. The nurse told me to undress and to put on the gown she had given me. One of the ties was missing at the back, but I wasn't going anywhere so it didn't really matter much. I still couldn't understand why I hadn't been taken to a ward as normal but this must have been how it was done if I was only having teeth out and who was I to question it. So here I was waiting to go to the theatre. The nurse came into the room again, read my name from the papers in her hand and I must admit I wasn't really listening to it seeing as I was the only one there. Then she said "Come with me." We were out in the corridor by now. I was holding the back of the gown trying to cover what dignity I had left when a very commanding voice almost shouted "Nurse what are you doing?" The young nurse said something while the older one ushered me back into the room, apologizing profusely at the same time. It seems there had been a mix up between me and another patient. The other nurse was now red with rage, telling the young nurse to get me a trolley quick and a theatre pack. The trolley was wheeled into the room. I was helped to get onto it and it was the best feeling in the world. The covers were so warm and comforting. They had obviously just come from a very warm cupboard. I was told to lay there and someone would come to me.

A new nurse appeared and she asked me what had happened. I told her what little I knew. While I was on the trolley I was given a pre-med injection. My mother was brought in to stay with me while the pre-med had a chance to work and to make sure that I didn't fall off the

Back row: Archie. Centre row: Kieth, myself and Ivy. Front row: Joyce and Michael - All my brothers and sisters I was caring for until my fifteenth birthday

Dad, Mum and sister Joyce at our front door

The blue dress. I had grown up !

trolley. At last I felt myself being wheeled to the operating theatre. I woke up to see an auxiliary nurse at the side of my bed. When I had come round a bit more she was smiling at me as she said "You're famous." I didn't understand what she meant. I asked her "Why?"

She asked me if I remembered what had happened that morning. I said "Yes I did." It appears that the nurse had picked up the wrong papers in the office and a woman with a similar name was coming in to have an ear infection investigated. She would have to go to the ear, nose and throat department and that is where the young nurse was taking me when we were stopped in our tracks. I said it might have been my fault for not hearing the name right. The nurse said "Oh, no. Not at all. There were two different times on the sheets and the other department doesn't open until later, so it was not your fault. No, you are famous for your flashing and vanishing act. In two seconds flat you were off the corridor and onto a trolley." We both started laughing and that's when I was reminded that I had no top teeth left.

I was still in hospital a few days later when I had to go down to the E.N.T. department. Those days I would be left to go on my own and I had to see Mr. Raynor. I was sat in the dental chair, looking out of the window and admiring the beautiful view over some corn fields. I could see a school on the brow of a hill. The school was High Storrs. We used to pass it on the way to Bents Green School. It felt so long ago now. A cheery "Hello" broke my pensive mood. It was Mr. Raynor and he was holding a familiar dish in his hand. He asked me how my mouth was and was it still swollen. I told him that it wasn't as bad as I thought it would feel and, with that, he said "Shall we try these in?" He reminded me that the palate would only be temporary. The now familiar command was given and I opened my mouth. I was surprised how easy they felt. There was a little soreness but nothing like what I had expected. I had to stay in until the next day. Mr. Raynor came to the ward the screens were drawn around the bed. He examined me and liked what he saw. He said "If I let you go home tonight will you go to see Mr. Hynes next week at the Royal hospital?" He gave me a time and day. I had to get a message home, but we had no phone. Only the richer people had telephones so, if there was a message of importance, we had to phone the English Steel works at the corner of the street. The gateman, as he was known, would pass the message on that I was ready to come home.

The following week I had the morning off work to go to the hospital. I put my make-up on. I was quite an expert nowadays, but my father was always telling me not to put a lot of that stuff on. I looked in the mirror. Temporary or not, my new teeth did wonders for my looks and right now I wasn't complaining. I arrived at the hospital in good time. As we sat waiting to go into the consulting room a nurse passed by whom I hadn't see for a while. She smiled, but she wasn't sure. I smiled back at her then she said "No it can't be. Nancy?" I got up from my seat. She couldn't believe how much I had grown "And just look at you. You are lovely." Mum and the nurse just small talked for a while. That nurse will never know how much she did for me in that one comment and, coupled with what Mr. Hynes said to me, it was a day I shall treasure. I went back to work with the broadest grin on my face. Mrs. Turner said "What's up with you? Have you won the pools?" I just shook my head and said nothing.

I had been at Woodhouse's for about two months when Mrs. Turner and I were called into the office early Monday morning. We were told that we would have to take a lesser job if we wanted to stay working there. Mrs. Turner was shocked and so was I, to say the least. She asked what was happening. The manager said that a new company was taking over the shop and would be bringing most of its existing staff with them and, seeing that they had got a cook and two assistants, our services would no longer be required. We asked what jobs were on offer. "The only jobs are cleaning jobs." was the reply.

I have never seen 'Mrs. T' angry before, but she was raging mad now, not only for herself, but for me as well. I could hear her saying "She is not going to be a cleaner, not at her age. She should be given something better and you know it." I as hoping she would be more careful in what she was saying, or both of us would be out of a job anyway. The boss was trying to calm her down by now. He was trying to convince her to take the job and in time she may get her old job back again at a later date, but Mrs. 'T' was having none of it. She just came back at him "With two assistants, what chance do you think she's got." Then she said "Give her her cards and let her go with a good reference. She is not going to be a cleaner."

I was mortified. My father would think that it was my fault that I got the sack. He definitely wouldn't believe what was happening here. I opened my mouth to say something but Mrs. T put her hand on my arm and said "You'll get another job in no time, you'll see if you don't. Now come on. Lets have a cup of tea while he writes your references out." I was shaking at the thought of having to go home and tell my father about this morning, but while we were having our tea, Mrs. T told me to go up to the employment office. It was less than a mile from where we were and they would give me some job cards. She said "If you go from here you will have time to go and see what jobs they've got to offer." The manager buzzed for us to go to his office. I was both frightened and sad at having to leave. I was given my cards with an apology from the manager. At the door Mrs. T gave me a kiss and said "You'll be all right lass" then she put me in the direction of the employment office. It was around nine thirty in the morning.

At the employment office I was given three job cards. It was around ten o'clock. One was not far from the office. It turned out to be one of the little mesters workshops that were in Sheffield. These places usually made knives, cutlery or scissors. The one I went to was typical of many. From the outside it looked filthy. I climbed the wooden plank steps leading to a dark brown dirty door. I rang the bell. The door was opened by a man dressed in a brown paper apron that was covered in oil. He was polite in his manner as he took me to a room that passed for an office. This room overlooked a scene out of a Dickens novel. At the far end of the workshop was an open fire. This had two functions; one to heat the whole room up and second, to heat the metal used for making what appeared to be pen knives, or small blade instruments. The noise was terrific after the comparative peacefulness of the kitchen I had just left. The few words that were said denoted that the job was mine. At first I would be expected to fetch and carry for the workers. To go and get what they wanted for dinner, mash tea and, in between, I would learn how to pack the crude blades ready for the next process. I would have to start work at seven o'clock on week days and eight o'clock Saturdays until twelve. As he was showing me out he was saying if you want the job be here by seven prompt. When I got outside I took the deepest breath and said "No thank you" but not to the boss. I was scared of him already.

From here I walked a mile across town to where Ansons umbrella factory was on Duke street. I knocked on a big door that didn't seem to be used much. I stepped back and waited for an answer but it didn't come. I decided to walk around the corner. There was a big gate with a smaller door in it. It was the same dark maroon colour as the front door was, but this little door had the hallmarks of being used regularly. I turned the big handle. I had to duck my head to get in through the door hole. Inside I found myself in a yard. I closed the door behind me then looked for signs of an office or reception. To the right in the far corner were the outside toilets. Before them and still to the right I saw a little plaque on a door it read 'Enquiries'. I looked over to my left and there was a two story building with sash windows. Each window was made up of eight little square panes of glass. There were four of these windows on the bottom and four on top, with two smaller windows to the right of these. I saw several faces looking at me from both the upstairs and the downstairs windows. It looked like a comedy show, because the people upstairs didn't know that the people downstairs were doing exactly the same. One of the chaps from the downstairs windows pointed towards the enquiry door. I thanked him in mime. As I turned I allowed myself to smile at the picture I had just seen. I went through the door to my right and was met by a woman who had just come down some stairs. I asked to see a Mr. Anson. She told me to wait a moment and in an instant a portly man came out of an office, held out his hand and, as we shook hands, he was saying "Come this way." I gave him the card from the employment office as he offered me a seat.

He asked me why I wanted to change jobs. I explained that I didn't want to leave but the circumstances didn't allow me to stay. He asked if I had got any references and I gave him the letter from Woodhouse's store, still sealed because the other boss hadn't asked for them. Mr. Anson took a few minutes to read it then he asked about the cook. He asked me to wait outside for a moment. When he called me in to his office again he asked me if I would like to have a look around. Without waiting for my answer he called the woman upstairs to come and take me to have a look around the place. I liked him. We went across the yard into the two story building. Now I was beginning to feel a bit shy because I had already seen them looking at me and now I was going to meet them.

We went into the downstairs work place first. There were about five men, all stood at a bench that ran along the window side of the room. They were making up the frames for the umbrellas. The two or three women I could see were sat down at benches twisting and cutting wires. They were all sure of hand and very quick. I was hoping that this wasn't the job on offer. I was sure they had mentioned sewing at the office, but I couldn't see any sewing being done here. However, the people were all very friendly. We went upstairs into the kitchen. It was a lot different to what I had just left that morning. It was bare except for a sink, a table, two benches and a cupboard. There was an old gas cooker. It looked like Mrs. Beaton might have learned to cook on it. There were also some old pans and a kettle. I noticed a not too hungry looking spider sat on a web in a corner on top of, what was very loosely named as, the pot cupboard.

We turned our back on the spider and the pot cupboard, went out of the door and across the top of the stairs into what was named the 'bale and cutting room'. In here there were all kinds of different cloths and materials for making up the umbrella canopies. There were silks, cottons and plastics and hung on the edges of the cutting benches were templates for different sized umbrellas, from a child's to a fishing umbrella. The umbrellas would come in eight ribbed up to sixteen ribbed styles. The sixteen ribbed were usually the fishing styles. There was the pagoda shape and the parasol. These would sometimes be made up with a frill around the edge for special occasions or for shows. Now I was becoming interested because I could hear sewing machines in the next room. We passed through a doorway, minus the door. In here we were greeted with a chorus of "Hello." I was introduced to Dorothy. She appeared to be the one in charge. She was portly with red cheeks, mainly due to the fact that she was stood right beside the open fire. Again this had two purposes, one was to heat the room and the other was to heat a steamer that would be used to get any excessive creasing out of the umbrellas. In a corner across from her were two sewing machines. A woman called Winnie was busy sewing the hems for the umbrellas. These would be done in long strips, sometimes as long as the bale of cloth itself. They were all girls in this room and the atmosphere felt very friendly and easy. I was shown the job I would be doing. It would be putting the gitts on the joints of the ribs to protect them from damp and rust. I would be seated next to a girl called Audrey Spooner and her sister Vera. I was told, as I was at the first place, that I would have to go for the dinners and mash the tea at break times and keep the kitchen clean. Now, I had just seen the kitchen and it would take a small miracle to get it clean in one go. As we turned to go out of the room Dorothy called to me "Tha'll be alreet 'ere lass." I was hooked. In the office

Mr. Anson said "Well, what do you think. Would you like the job?" I nod my head and said, "Yes please." When he said "Can you start this afternoon?" a hundred emotions went through me. I was surprised by the question. I was exited at getting the job so quickly and what would I tell my parents? I was told to come back at one o'clock that day. We shook hands and I was back on the street.

I had been given a watch for Christmas and, as I looked at it, I could see that I had about one and half hours to kill. I couldn't go home, it was too far. I had got my bus fare home, but no money for any dinner. I used to get my dinners free at Woodhouse's ,but not any more. I had got another job now and in the mean time I had to make a decision; should I spend my bus fare home on some crisps or go hungry for the rest of the day. I decided to walk home and buy the crisps. I knew the area because we were not far from Maud Maxfield school and I knew my way to the peace gardens. Though it was a cold day it was bright and sunny. I found myself a place to sit out of the wind. I admired the view over Sheffield looking out towards the moors on the other side. It was surprising how far you could see on a day like this and it was surprising how slow time went when you were wanting it to go. It was just gone twelve fifteen. I decided to take a walk around the grounds. The monument in the Peace Gardens is in memory of the people of Eyam who, in 1665, were ravaged with the plague. They incarcerated themselves so that the plague would spread no further. No fewer than 250 people were to perish. One of the last to die was the Reverend Mompesson's wife, Katherine.

I had finished my walk and had finished my crisps, so I started to walk back to Ansons. I got there about fifteen minutes early. I knocked on the office door. There was no answer so I made my way across the yard and climbed the stairs towards the voices in the kitchen. I knocked on the door and, as soon as I had done so, I felt stupid because this was where I was to work. Now, milder than ever, I entered. Dorothy was one of the first faces I recognised. I explained that there was no one in the office yet and with one accord two or three answered that they would be out at dinner. I was asked if I would like a cup of tea. Any other day I might have refused, but today was not one of them. At one o'clock on the dot everyone got up from their seats. Some washed their cups in the sink and the others just went out with the little bit that was left in the bottom of the cup. Dorothy indicated that I should follow her. We went into the covering room, as it was known. She told me to sit down. I was sat next to an empty chair but, two minutes later, the Spooner sisters came in with an apology to Dorothy. She was definitely in charge.

She picked up the phone on her bench and she said "Is Mr. Anson, or Michael there?" Then I heard her say "Yes she's here." She put the phone down and told me to go to the office. When I got to the office I was surprised to see a much younger version of Mr. Anson. I assumed this must be his son. He introduced himself "Mr. Anson, but to save confusion, I am known as Mr. Michael around here." He had a very nice smile and so had I when I reported for my job in my new employment.

When I got home that night it was much the same time as usual, so Mum didn't notice any thing had changed. However, I knew that I would have to tell her before morning because I would have to get up earlier. I decided to wait until after tea then Dad would be asleep in the chair and we would be in the kitchen.

"I don't work at Woodhouse's any more Mum" I told her. "What do you mean 'Nanc, I mean, Anne." she replied. "I've got another job." "Where, and why. What's happened?" she asked and with my back to the sink I started to tell her the tale of the day. When I had finished she was relieved that I hadn't got the sack for any other reasons. Then she went on to say "Don't tell your Dad yet Nancy. I'll tell him later." I told her that I would be getting a bit more money with this work. She gave me one of her knowing looks then said "Let's keep that to ourselves for a bit love."

I was happy working here. I liked the work and started by sewing little covers on the joints of the umbrella frames. These covers were called 'gitts'. At first I thought they were pulling my leg. I had heard about this sort of leg pulling. However, when I read it on a box, and was satisfied. For a long time it embarrassed me to have to ask for 'gitts' from the stores.

At fifteen starting a new job meant being the errand girl. I had to walk up and down Duke street but, in this case, I walked down the hill first then back up again. I did it in rain, hail or shine and the chips had to be bought from a certain chip shop, or I would know about it. Across from the chip shop was Gunston's bakeries. I have bought pounds of their cream biscuits, all in two ounce or half pound lots, depending on the day. On Fridays I would be given a tip or treated to a bun or someone would buy me my dinner. They were very good to me, but the one thing I would not fetch were cigarettes. They tried to coax me; they tried to tell me it was my job to fetch what ever they needed, they threatened me with the sack, but only by way of a joke. However, one man did ask Mr. Anson about my right to refuse. Mr. Anson asked why I was so adamant about not getting the cigarettes. My reply was that I didn't smoke and most of the people who were asking me to get them had been into a paper shop that morning or in a pub the night before. Apart from me not smoking, why didn't they get a packet then? He just smiled and said "I must admit you have a point there Anne." The following day, while we were all in the kitchen, Mr. Michael came in and said "Anne is under no obligation to fetch cigarettes for anyone. If you find that you need any you can ask permission from your charge-hand to go out and get some." I could feel all their eyes on me. Then the discussion started; was he right or was he wrong? I must admit they were all very good about it all when the smoke cleared, if you will excuse me the pun.

I got my chance to go on the sewing machines when Connie the machinist went off ill. I was asked if I could work one. I said a tentative yes, but I wasn't sure. I had used the one at school and Connie had let me have a go on hers in our break times and I did get the hang of using a hemmer. The work was piling up and they needed some -one quick. In those days there was no training or guide lines to work to. If you said you could do a job you just got on with it. I was surprised how quickly I got into it. When Connie came back I was asked if I would like to hem the heavier cloths, such as canvass for the fishing umbrellas and heavy duty cloth for the industrial umbrellas. I jumped at the chance. It was no trouble to me to hem thirty yards of material at one go.

I had been at Ansons for a few months when a new girl started. She was around seventeen. She was a bit bigger than myself and when I wasn't on the machine I sat at the side of her. We would share the gitt covers and cottons, needles, etc. After a few days she asked me to get her some cigarettes. She had been told that I didn't fetch them, but she insisted that it was my job to get what she wanted. I told her where the office door was if she wanted to make an argument out of it. She wasn't happy, but she didn't go to the office either. Afterwards she started to make things difficult for me. Over a number of weeks she would leave the boxes empty of whatever we needed. She would never fill them up. She would make some petty excuse, like she didn't notice that they were empty, or the colour of the umbrella had changed and we would need new cottons. She would conveniently find that she had to go somewhere quick. She wasn't very well liked and, though I didn't say anything, people were not blind, especially Dorothy. One day Irene went too far even for me. She asked me to get some things for her from a shop that wasn't on the route I took. I got an idea she was doing it on purpose, but I couldn't think why. I was too innocent to put two and two together. The thing was that she wanted an argument. She started by saying "First you won't fetch cigs, now you won't get these. Who do you think you are? Miss prim and proper. You're certainly not prim and tha' don't look proper to me." Then a few other derogatory remarks followed. I knew that if I started a fight in here I would lose my job. So I decided to bide my time. Dorothy could see the situation was getting bad, but she said nothing. From where I sat I could see her. She was shaking her head, but indicated that it was all right outside. I bide my time and when five o'clock came, I was outside waiting.

It doesn't take long for news to get around when something is about to happen. With my workmates supporting and encouraging me to give her one for them, the job became easier. I didn't want to fight this girl though I knew how to. Being brought up in a district like Attercliffe and, having four brothers, I would be marked as a coward if I didn't carry out my threat. So here I was, waiting for this girl. The fight was short but not too sweet. I knew the job was done when I saw her sitting on the floor with her back to the wall. I leaned over her and said "If you ever call me again, remember today!"

I walked home that day and I was crying, not for myself, but in temper. For her to say those things about me was an attack on my mother and all the hardship that she has had to endure in the past. No, there was a job to be done and I had just done it.

When I arrived at work the next day I was a mini hero. I remember feeling a bit embarrassed about it. When Irene came in Dorothy told her she had been moved to another department with some lame excuse that they were short staffed in there. It wasn't long before I was called into the office. As I knocked on the office door I heard Mr. Ansons voice "Come in." I stood there thinking about the headmaster incident. He came from behind his desk saying "I hope your not going to make a habit of this fighting lark Anne." As he looked at me I could tell he knew that I had no choice. Then with a few more words in my ear he opened the door and, with a pat on my shoulder, he said "We won't hear any more about it will we Anne? Good morning then." It was a big relief to know that I had still got my job. Soon after this episode Irene left.

I made long lasting friendships with the two Spooner sisters and a girl named Barbara Truelove. She had a brother who was in the army and whom I was destined to meet one day. We three would go to the pictures together and our love of dancing was mutual. We would go dancing at the Embassy dance hall most Saturday nights.

I had been going back to Fulwood Annex once a week for three weeks now, so my new teeth should be ready very soon. When I got into the dentists chair, Mr. Raynor brought out my new teeth. They looked rather large at the side of what I had been used to. He fitted them in and the usual adjustments had to be made. He gave me a mirror and said "Now what do you think of those?" as he asked me to smile by demonstrating the act himself. I was amazed. The temporary ones were nice but these were better. The top of the palate had been raised filling the void that was in the roof of my mouth so now the nasal speech had all but gone. Yes, I liked what I saw looking back at me from the mirror. I left the surgery knowing I had one more visit before I got a new and permanent look. Mr. Raynor had asked me to bring my Mother with me the next week. He added that Mr. Hynes may be here to have a look at the work we have done.

The following week we were walking down the drive to the Annex and we took time to stop and look at the view we had seen so many times. Mum said "How many years have we been coming here Nanc?" It was at times like this that Mum would revert back to my old name. I didn't mind and it felt right some how. "It will be ten years next year." I replied. "As long as that? Yes I suppose it must be." We looked over the valley. In ten years the view was much the same as it was then; breathtakingly beautiful. We arrived at the E.N.T. department with time to spare. I had been told to wear my make up on this occasion, a thing I didn't always do when I knew that I would be asked to remove it before I had treatment, but for some reason I was asked to wear it today. A nurse called my mother and I into the treatment room and Mum was offered a chair. Mr. Raynor came in and handed me the

Una (top), Barbara and myself (middle) between the Spooner sisters

palate saying "Put them in Annie?", my christened name. He gave me the mirror and said "What do you think now?"

I was almost sixteen years old. I turned, looked at my mother and smiled. She didn't have to say anything. Her eyes were beginning to fill, but her smile spoke volumes as she searched for her handkerchief that was in her pocket. Mr. Raynor left the room and returned in a little while to tell us that Mr. Hynes had just arrived and would be here very soon. The man himself came into the surgery. He had two other men with him. He said "Hello" to Mum and then he turned to me. "Now Annie how are you?" I was surprised how well I spoke back to him. He turned to the two men and introduced them by name then he said "You don't remember these two gentlemen, but they saw you at the Grand Hotel in Sheffield when you were about eleven years old, I think." He was right. I didn't remember them, but I did remember when he asked me to speak without teeth. I was hoping he wasn't going to repeat the request because, this time, I might just refuse him for once. He turned to the two men and said "What do you think of our young lady now?" The two of them nodded in unison. "The change is tremendous." They started talking as if I had just left the room. "You have done a wonderful job Mr. Hynes." " Do you intend to do any more? With Annie I mean." This type of conversation went on for a few more minutes, then it was as if someone had put a penny in the slot and they remembered that I was still there. Mr. Hynes apologized for his ignorance and left the room. After this I recall seeing him only twice more. Mr. Raynor was to be my dentist until I was about twenty-five years old.

I was beginning to go dancing more regularly now. On Tuesdays it would be to the club and on Thursdays to the Embassy dance hall. I was gaining confidence in my new look, bought one or two new dresses and was encouraged by my friends to put on a little more make up, like eye liner and rouge. I had my hair cut and done in the new feather look. I wasn't sure if I liked it, but I got the reassurance that it suited me. So my passage into womanhood had begun.

1953 was a very eventful year. It was the year rationing ended. I saw a barrow loaded with thousands of bananas on it. The next day I went and bought four for Mum. I think that was the maximum I could get in one buy. I remember seeing long queues at the sweet shops. Every one was queuing for chocolate it seemed. The shops themselves were rationing the sweets; only so much to each sale. The Government was talking of rationing if people didn't stop the frantic buying that was going on. In this year Queen Elizabeth the second was crowned. The king had died on February 6th 1952. So with the coronation in June, it felt like a new beginning; a second new year if you like. The films were now being made in Technicolor. My first epic film was 'The Robe'. I saw this film three times. On one of these occasions I took my grandmother to see it.

The year ended with a very good round of parties, dances and long walks home, because we had missed the last bus. I still had my share of baby sitting to do, because my youngest sister, Joyce, was only six. However, if I mentioned to Kerkhoff that there was some party or date happening and I couldn't go because I had to baby sit, she would step in and offer to do it for me. She was a wonderful neighbour.

A few weeks into the new year, Barbara asked me if I would like to write to her brother who was in the army. He was nineteen and stationed in Germany. I wasn't sure at first, but she had told me that his old girlfriend had gone off with someone else, so he was feeling a bit down and wanted some new pen friends. I started writing to him on a letter wrote, letter received basis. We got to know each other's likes and dislikes. He had a good job waiting for him when he had completed his National Service. During this time I still went out dancing. I kept very good friends with Dorothy and I was introduced to the family friends by his mother as "The girl who is writing to our Herbert." However, we all knew him as Bert. The letters became more frequent and more intimate. I sent him a photograph and he sent me his, but by this time I could have recognized him in a crowd of thousands just by the photographs his Mum had already shown me. He would have been very embarrassed to know I had seen him with no clothes on at the age of six months, so I never told him.

At Ansons there was quite a lot of joke-sharing and laughter. One of the biggest laughs was provided by Minnie. She was a slight person and liked her cigarettes. She sat in her own little corner and got away with murder at times and Dorothy turned a blind eye, very often, to the delight of others. On the day in mind, Dorothy and Minnie were enjoying a crafty smoke with their mid-morning tea and Dorothy was supposed to be looking out for Mr. Anson, because smoking was definitely not allowed in the covering room. We were all talking at the same time and trying to put our point across on some issue or other. Dorothy took

Mum and Mrs. Kerkhoff on Pinstone Street, late 1950's

Back Row left to right: Mum, myself and Mrs. Kerkhoff, 1953. The rest are other family and friends. Note the V for victory sign drawn on the wall on the right

her eyes off the window to add her two penn'orth to the argument. This proved a disastrous move. We could hear 'his' voice coming up the stairs. Dorothy's cigarette went on the fire, while Minnie flipped hers, then through it in the drawer. While Mr. 'A' was talking to Dorothy, Minnie realized that there was smoke coming out of the drawer and those of us that could see it were beginning to deteriorate into hidden fits of suppressed laughter. Minnie picked up her half cup of tea and threw the lot into the drawer, cup and all, opening and shutting it in a blink of an eye. Some one passed her another and she repeated the action. Dorothy was aware of what was happening behind Mr. 'A's back and was now edging him towards the doorway, with no door, taking care to keep Mr. 'A' in tight conversation while they crossed the room. Mr. Anson's parting words to Dorothy were "That fire's smelling a bit strong today Dorothy. I should keep an eye on it if I were you."

When he was finally out of earshot it was as if a balloon had burst. We all fell about laughing, whilst Minnie produced the soggy contents of her drawer, some of which had leaked onto her lap and down her lyle stockinged legs. The sight was hilarious to say the least and, needless to say, there was definitely no more smoking upstairs.

Audrey Spooner and I were good friends. We were both writing to boys who were in the forces. She had known hers before he went away and she had seen Bert when he had been on leave and assured me that he was all right, and that I would like him when I met him. I had mixed feelings about the prospects of meeting him. One of the last letters I had from him was to tell me that our letter writing days were nearly over because he was coming home in two weeks time. I read that letter over and over. I didn't want to believe it, because I feared the consequences. He had never seen me only in the photograph I had so carefully chosen. We had been writing to each other for ten months and I was as nervous as a child on a high wall. I had a feeling that I was about to fall off my wall.

His Mum had arranged tea for us on the day we planned to meet. I was to go up to his house. I was on the bus that would take me to the end of the street where he lived. I was sweating though it was late October. I could see the stop I had to get off at. I really had the urge to stay on the bus. But I thought about his Mum and the effort she would have put into the tea she was doing. So I got off, I crossed the road;

then I heard a man call my name. He was a little way down the road. I knew instinctively who he was. As he came nearer I could see he was tanned, about as tall as I was and he was broad, broader than I thought he would be. I was thankful that he wasn't a small man, like his father. We shook hands and he said "Shall we have a walk?" I was so grateful that he had saved me from the embarrassment of having to meet him in front of his entire family. I found out later from Barbara that he had asked her to walk him up to the bus stop and leave him when I got there. By the time we got to his house we were talking as if we had known each other for years.

I had been writing to him for ten months. Little did I realise that it would be over by Christmas. The first two weeks that he was home were a whirlwind. We went everywhere. I had taken a week off work so that we could spend as much time as possible getting to know each other. My father got him a membership to the working mens clubs and we spent a couple of nights in their company. We really did get on well together. On the Monday of the third week we arranged to meet. Barbara came to work and told me that Bert would phone me later on in the morning. We weren't supposed to have phone calls at work, only in emergencies. So, when the call came I was allowed to take it, but to tell the person on the other end not to make a habit of it. He apologized for not going out and said that he might not make it until Friday and he would see me then. In the meantime he would send me a letter with Barbara. We met on Friday as arranged but something was wrong. He made me laugh and we enjoyed the night out, but there was something not right.

The next day, Saturday, he asked me if I wanted to go to the football match. I used to go to them with two of my aunties, so I was more than happy to go with him. On our way home we had some chips and fish and ate them in the street, out of the newspaper. I hadn't done that for a long time, only at the seaside. It was around half past six when we got to his house. He complained of not feeling well, and said it might be the chips we had just eaten, but I felt all right. He said he felt like going to bed to see if that would do him any good. He indicated that I should go home by way of getting my coat as he was saying "I'll walk you to the bus stop." "Don't bother. Get yourself to bed and come down to me tomorrow afternoon" I replied.

It was four o'clock on Sunday afternoon. I was wearing the little satin suit that he had brought back from Germany. There was a knock at the door and my dad shouted "Come in lad. You don't have to knock" but the door didn't open. Instead there was another knock and my brother opened the door this time. I could see it was Robert, Bert's younger brother. The letter he gave me said "Meet me tonight for five minutes at the top of your road. I have something to tell you." I didn't go and he didn't call. Barbara and I still remained firm friends. She told me that his first girlfriend had come on the scene again and Bert wanted to give it another chance. I could tell that she was very annoyed at what he had done to me. I asked her not to fall out with him. After all, he was her brother and I didn't know him that well. She told me that the family weren't all that keen on this girl, but it was his choice. So I made my mind up not to dwell on the matter any longer and put it down to experience.

Almost a month to the day since we parted company Barbara gave me a letter from Bert. It said "I will call for you at your house tonight." Then he went on with a whole sentence of apologies. I thanked her for the note. "What shall I tell Bert?" Barbara asked. I said "Just tell him that you gave me the note" and left it at that.

I got home from work and I asked Mum if she was going out. I knew Dad was on nights so there was no worry about that. The letter said he would be here about seven thirty. If Mum was going to the pictures, as she did sometimes on Tuesdays, I would have the house to myself for at least an hour. As he knocked on the door it shattered the peacefulness of the room. I let him in and he sat down. He said he was sorry for leaving me. He put a parcel on the table. I told him that I wasn't afraid to tell him to his face that I wasn't interested in him any more. I wanted to tell him that I wasn't a coward who sent letters with my brothers and sisters. It didn't please me to see the hurt in his face, but *he* wasn't going to tell me to be in when ever it suited *him*. He asked me to go back with him, but I said "No." He left leaving behind a large box of chocolates. I shared these out with the family. Bert got married a year later to the same girl.

CHAPTER 6

VENGEANCE CAN BE SWEET

1954 was a very eventful year. Barbara started going out with a boyfriend, so we saw less of her. Audrey had decided to get married to her boyfriend, Gordon, when he got out of the army. I had a wonderful holiday in Wales with a couple I called Aunt and Uncle. They had no children of their own, so they looked on me as the daughter they hadn't got. It was only my second holiday. The first was when I was fifteen years old. I went to London with a couple called Margaret and Norman. They had a little girl and they said I could go if I would baby sit for them at nights. I thought it was a lovely exchange; a holiday for a few hours baby sitting, but it didn't turn out like that. The baby sitting was only a little white lie, so that my father wouldn't refuse his mate a baby sitter. The fact of the matter was that he would have refused me a holiday as such. The sad thing was I couldn't talk about the wonderful nights I had out in London; I had danced to the Joe Loss band twice, I had been to see a West End show and numerous other outings. I did tell my Mother the truth about the holiday, but not until I was married.

I started a new job in this year. Old Mr. Anson had retired and Mr. Michael had taken over the business. He had been told that a compulsory purchase order was being issued on some factories and houses in the park area, and that his factory would be one of them. Although the purchase wasn't imminent, we were told to take any job that we might be offered and an unbiased reference would be given. My new place of work was Resco's, a sewing place making mens shirts, lingerie, and baby wear. It was at the top of the road from where I lived. Again it was a small family business run by Mr. Resser and his daughter. When my sister left school she got a job at the same place. It was common practice for members of the same family to end up working together

I was beginning to lose touch with Barbara and Vera, Audrey's sister. However, Audrey and I were still firm friends. I didn't see much of my friends from the Radical Club now. I had struck up a new friendship with a girl named Brenda. We almost got ourselves evicted from church. It was coming up to Easter and Brenda was a Sunday school teacher. She asked if I would help her with the children when she had to take them to the Easter service, which was to be held in the main church. I said that I would be more than happy to help her. We put two of the children between us, a few were in front and the rest either side of us. We were seated near the front of the church. The service was going well until we started to sing the hymn 'Jesus Christ is risen today, Haaaaliloo,oo,oo,ya. On the second Haaaaliloo,oo,oo,ya we turned simultaneously, looked straight at each other with our mouths wide open, saw the funny side of it and started to laugh in the middle of it. The two girls between us started to giggle and this started a contagious infection. It was all right while the hymn was going on, trying to stifle the giggles, but when the hymn stopped and it was time for the prayers, the silence that should have prevailed was peppered with unsuccessfully smothered giggles. No amount of reverent feeling could stop it. We were approached by the verger to kindly keep the children quieter or we would have to leave. I can't hear the hymn now without a little smile on my face and it's not only because Jesus Christ is risen today.

When Audrey's boyfriend, Gordon, was demobbed from the army, I began to see less of her and more of Brenda and Louise. Louise was one of Brenda's work mates, but we had seen each other at the occasional dance.

My eldest brother was called up to do his national service in 1955. Apart from the loss of wages from a house that could ill afford it, it nearly broke my Mother's heart. She was remembering Dad when he was in uniform. "You're the image of your Father" she would say to my brother. "I'm so glad for you that there isn't a war on, son."

After many months of not seeing Audrey she phoned me and said that she wanted to see me. She wouldn't tell me what it was about, but she asked me to meet her in a pub in town. It was all a bit of a mystery why she wanted to see me now. When I arrived at the pub, Barbara and

Left to right: Vera Spooner, Barry Wragg, myself, Audrey Spooner, Barbara Truelove and her boyfriend, taken at the Embassy Dance Hall, Sheffield. We were a group for approximately two years

Myself and Audrey Spooner

Vera were there. We sorted the drinks out and then Audrey said "Now that we are all here I can tell you. I'm going to get married in three months time and I want you all to be my bridesmaids." We were all astounded because none of us, not even her sister Vera, knew what she was up to. It turned out to be a memorable night. The wedding day was wonderful. Audrey had chosen to have a rainbow wedding. She was in a delicate cream and the five bridesmaids were in different shades of pastel colours. She had invited my mother and my brother managed to get leave from the army to be there. It turned out be an unforgettable day.

Brenda, Louise and myself had been going out together for about a year when we went to the Cutlers Hall. This place was very upmarket and still is. It is the official office and banqueting suite for the Master Cutler of Sheffield. So, to go there was a very grand feeling. I had been dancing with a boy I liked very much. In the middle of one dance he asked if he could take me out and I said "Yes." We made a date and time to meet. We agreed to meet at the C&A stores on the high street. I got there ten minutes before the agreed time of seven o'clock. Seven o'clock came and went and so did fifteen minutes past. As it got towards half past I was hoping that I had got it wrong and that the time for meeting was seven thirty. I didn't wait for the Cathedral clock to tell me that it was seven thirty. I just slipped away as inconspicuously as I could and hoped that no-one had seen me waiting there. When I saw him at the dance the following Thursday he was full of apologies and made some excuses. He said that he would make it up to me if only I give him the chance. We made arrangements to meet at Coles corner, a popular meeting place in Sheffield. This time I was sure he would be there, but at seven fifteen I left. I was so angry now. I didn't go home, but went to the pictures. I was too angry to get involved with the film. When I got home Mum said "Hello love. Had a nice time?" " Yes thanks Mum, but I'm tired. Good night." I replied.

Because I shared the bed with my sister, I couldn't do the only thing that I felt like doing and that was to have a good cry. I felt so alone. I was so sure, but now I couldn't even tell Mum how I felt and how rejected I was feeling. There was no place of privacy in a crowded home to vent my private feelings. Within my mixed up feelings there was one thing creeping up on me and that was vengeance. I wanted to get my own back if it was only to gain a little self satisfaction. So, I made my mind up to go to the dance that week. I saw him and made a point of going to the other side of the room. When all the dancers were on the floor he made his way towards me. I felt like screaming at him to go away, but he sat at the side of me and put a drink in front of me as he said "I suppose I've blown it, but I had to work late." Then he went on a little too much to be convincing. I reminded him that he knew where I lived and that I could read a letter, and that they did have a phone at work. He apologized again then he said "I don't suppose you want to go out with me again do you." I said "I might." I could see he was taken aback by this. By the end of the night I was going to meet him on Saturday outside C&A stores. I saw Brenda the following night and asked her if she would like to go to see a film at the Gaumont cinema. She was a bit taken aback on the choice of film. It was a gangster, but she agreed. We got on the tram at ten to seven. This would be passing C&A stores at just gone seven o'clock. Brenda was sat next to the window and, as we passed the shop, I leaned over, looked out of the window and said to Brenda "See that man there?. He's waiting for me." She recognized him and looked in disbelief at me. I said "Don't worry. We're still going to the pictures. *He* can wait for *me* now."

I was determined to go to the Cutlers Hall that Thursday night though I wasn't looking forward to it one bit. I was longer than usual changing my shoes and told the others to go on without me. To climb the staircase at the 'Hall' gives you a grand feeling, but that night it felt like I was climbing the gallows. I was sure there would be a row. I turned into the dance hall to be met by him. They had obviously told him I was here. I was shocked and relieved when he put his hand out to me and said "Put it there and lets call it quits." Then he added, tongue in cheek, "Do you want to try again?" Laughing now I said "Not likely." We stayed friends and my dignity was still intact.

With Audrey's wedding out of the way we seemed to just drift apart more than ever. A few months after the fun and games around C&A I met Reg. He wasn't handsome, but he was kind and loving. He had a good job but I was to find out that he was the biggest liar this side of God's earth. However, I was in love. He told me that he had a good job and, by way of proving it, he taught me how to use a micrometer, a small tool to measure millionths of inches. His parents lived in Wisbech and I was invited to meet his parents at their home. They were lovely people and very welcoming towards me. I later went to Lands End with them and that period was when I saw Stonehenge at four o'clock in the morning. I would have much rather stayed asleep. Reg wouldn't tell me where he worked. When I asked he would just say "It's in Ecclesall" or "You're not going to have to go there are you?" So the matter just drifted into another conversation. We got into a pattern of meeting regularly during the week, but he would never meet me on Sunday morning. When Mum found out that he lived away she started to invite him down for Sunday lunch. At first he would come and stay all day and we would go out in the evening. As the weeks went by he started to turn up just as the meal was ready for the table then he would stay for a couple of hours, make his excuses and go. I could see it was irritating my parents and it did seem that he was beginning to take me for granted.

I asked him why he would never go out on a Sunday morning. He turned very secretive and said "If I tell you, will you not tell anyone?" I more than agreed. He told me he was taking flying lessons. When I asked him why he wanted it kept a secret he said that he wanted it to be a surprise for his parents. He didn't want any of his mates to know either. Well, that part would be easy as I had only met one of his 'many' mates and that was a 'Hello, good bye' situation. I asked him to show me his flyers log book, a thing that every flyer is proud of, but he kept forgetting it. I suggested that we went back to his digs for him to get it. He just said that it was a bit of a journey just for a book. "Don't you believe that I'm taking lessons?" he would say. So I agreed that it was a long way to just look at a book.

He promised to take me with him one day when he got a bit better at it. I asked him to take a photograph of the plane, needless to say that never came. I asked him to take me with him the next Sunday. He said that the car he went in was full of the other fellows who were training. We had been going together for almost eighteen months. We had got engaged on the anniversary of our first meeting. Reg would stay over night at our house if the weather was bad, or if we had arrived home too late for him to get home. Apparently the landlady bolted the door at twelve o'clock. He would sleep on the settee. On one of these nights, Reg had gone to the toilet and I was making the bed up. I let his jacket fall to the floor. His things fell out of his inside pocket, including the book he said he never carried because of the chance of losing it. It was our bank book. We had opened a joint account as we were saving for a house and wedding. I opened it expecting to see around three hundred pounds, but I was shocked to see only ninety pounds and some pennies. When he came back I didn't say anything to him. I kissed him good night then when to bed.

The next day I gave him a pound as an opener to my question; "By the way, how much have we got saved now?" he replied with some ridiculous figure, then I asked him to come out with me for once on Sunday morning. He said "You know I can't. If I miss a lesson it's a lot of money down the drain." I just said OK and left it at that. I was up early the next day, determined to be proved right or wrong. I caught a tram to town and then another to Ecclesall Road. It was nine thirty in the morning. I wasn't sure if the trams would go up that way at this time on a Sunday morning. I asked the conductor of the tram. He said "No, but this one would go past the bottom of that road." That would do and half an hour later I was walking up Ecclesall Road. I knew his address having copied it from one of the envelopes in his pocket. I knocked on the door of his lodgings and asked if Reg had gone out. She smiled and said "Reg, he never gets up early on Sunday morning love. Are you his girlfriend?" I said "Yes" Well I don't allow girls into the rooms, but if you like I'll tell him you're here. You can wait in the hall." I declined the offer and added "Are you sure he doesn't take flying lessons on Sunday mornings." She laughed out loud "No, not our Reg." I asked her not to tell him that I had been and with a knowing look she said "Don't worry lass. I haven't seen yer."

He came to dinner as usual, but I said that I would like to stay in for the rest of the day. I said that I wasn't feeling too good and asked him if he minded going. He said that he would come and see me tomorrow. I asked him to make it Tuesday. Why change the habit of a life time? I thought to myself. When he had gone I went upstairs and, with the bank book I had taken out of his pocket in my hands, I cried. Mum heard me. She came up and I told her the whole story and what a liar he was. I asked her to make sure that the house was empty on Tuesday night.

I didn't go to work on Tuesday. Instead I went to the bank and drew all the money out and closed the account. I packed all the engagement presents that had been bought by his side of the family into two bags. I took my ring off and put it back in it's box. I put both the ring and the bank book on top of the bags and waited. He knocked on the door and

Ivy (left) aged 16 and myself aged 20, taken at Cleethorpes 6th August 1958

walked in. I asked "Have you got the bank book?" and when he said "No" I asked "What's it like to be telling the truth for a change?" "What do you mean?" he replied. I told him to feel in his pocket. He was dumbfounded when he looked up and saw it in my hand. "And if you're going to take flying lessons you'll have to start getting up a lot earlier on Sundays." As he opened his mouth to speak I said "Don't bother. Here, take these and just go." He was outside before he could tell me any more lies.

After this, my moral feelings went right down. I began to wonder if it was me. Did I attract the wrong sort? Was it always going to be like this? I was still going out with my friends, but now I would make excuses not to go into town, not even to the pictures and, being the friends that they were, they could see what was happening. I was going into a depressive state. I would be twenty-one in November and I wasn't looking forward to it at all. I suddenly felt very old. I was so lucky to have friends who didn't just walk away. They were still there when I was ready to get back into the land of the living.

Brenda was going out with a boyfriend so we didn't see much of her now. Louise and the second Barbara proved to be good friends in need. We started to go out as we used to do and literally enjoyed life again. Brenda would try to get away from her boyfriend who was proving to be very possessive towards her. When she did get away we were the carefree threesome again.

My Twenty-first birthday was a day to remember; I had my second birthday cake. The first one was when I was eighteen. I didn't have a party then, only a small tea. We invited Grandma. Well, she did bake the cake. However, today I had two parties; one for the family at home and, in the evening, I took sandwiches and cakes to the Museum Pub. We spent some of the night in there and the rest of the night in the dance halls. It was a good day.

My brother Keith had started Saturday morning work at a garage. He had been working there for a couple of months. Once or twice I had stopped to chat to him as I passed the place so I knew one or two of the lads who worked there. Christmas came again and was once again a round of dancing and parties. After the festive season was over we settled back into our normal routine of the good life.

It was just after Christmas when Keith came home with a message from one of the chaps at work. He wanted to go out with me. I knew him by sight so I said that I would think about it. I wasn't sure if wanted to go out with anyone again. I was still hurting from Reg. Keith brought me a couple of messages from this guy. I gave in and we met for a night out. I met him in the pub at the top of the road where I lived. As we left the there was a car parked in front of the door. He opened the door for me and I got in. We went to the pictures and when we came out it was too late to go to the pub for a last drink so he drove me home. He stopped the car some distance away from the house and turned the engine off. It had been a pleasant evening and he had said the same. However, what he said a few seconds later crushed me. He said "I'm glad I had that bet." I asked him what he meant. "I went out with you for a bet." he replied.

I sat there a for what seemed an age as it sank in. That is why he wanted to meet me in the pub, and that is why one or two of his friends were there when I turned up. I turned to face him, and my hand went straight across his face. I could see from the light in the car I had made his eyes water. After I had hit him I just sat there. To this day I don't know why I didn't try to get out of the car as quickly as possible. I expected to be strangled, killed or, at the very least, slapped back. Instead, he reached over, opened the passenger door and indicated that I should leave. I walked the streets not wanting to go home. I didn't even care if someone got hold of me. When I arrived home I was thankful that all the lights were off and everyone was in bed. I dared not tell my brother what had happened or there would have been gang warfare. My three brothers, who were all tall and muscular, would have murdered him. So I didn't tell anyone until years later. It reminded me how cruel people can be. I was determined this time that an idiot like him wasn't going to take away from me what I had built up in the last few months. I went on with my life as if nothing had happened.

Soon after this episode my worst nightmare happened. I think the Gods were ganging up on me at this time in my life. I must say, though, that whenever we look back to this time it seems ridiculously funny now. I was getting ready for work one morning, late as usual. My sister had started work at the same place as I, so we were both in a hurry. She had been at the sink for what had seemed a tantalizingly long time so, when she had done, I was even later. I took out my palate, a thing I had done a thousand times, and started to brush it. Then it happened; there in the stone sink were two halves of the palate. I was mortified. I just stood looking at them. I was slowly convincing myself that they were broken. I had broken them only once before when I was about eight years old. However, that paled into insignificance compared to this. I contained my panic with the thought that I had saved my old ones somewhere in the house. I went upstairs and woke Mum. Dad had gone to work so she was on her own. It took her a few minutes to come round and realize just what she was looking at. She took the two bits from me saying "Oh, Nanc. What have you done?" I asked Mum to tell Ivy not to tell them the truth at work and to just say that I was ill. As Mum started to get dressed she said "We'll find your old ones out. You'll be all right. Put the kettle on, there's a love."

I looked in the drawer, I was sure they were in there. I looked in other places as well, but I could not find the elusive palate. Now, this was becoming serious and I was just a bit more than a little worried. "Go and have another look love, I'm sure they are there some where" Mum said. As Mum drank her tea she was looking as well. We gave up after half an hour. There were no more places to search.

The younger end of the family started to get up for school. I disappeared upstairs. They had never seen me without my teeth and this was not going to be the first time if I could help it. So, I went upstairs and made the beds until the house was empty again. When Mum got back from taking the young ones to school she told me that she had telephoned the hospital and they had told her to take the palate to a dentist on Attercliffe. They would repair them temporarily, but we couldn't go until eleven o'clock. That would give the hospital time to phone the dentist and explain the urgency for the teeth.

As we walked into the surgery the receptionist looked up "Ah, you must be Annie." It was a bit off-putting to realize that I could be recognized just by being looked at. I must say I didn't like that feeling very much. The dentist came into the room. He was a bit more diplomatic. He looked on a pad as he was saying " You're the young lady who has had the accident?" I gave him the two bits wrapped in white gauze. He looked at them fitting the two halves together, his head was giving little short nods. "Yes, I think we can manage that, but I will have to keep them until tomorrow dinner- time. If you call around one o'clock they should be ready for you."

As we left the dental surgery we met one of the neighbours. It was winter so it wasn't unusual to see someone muffled up in a scarf that reached to her ears. However, our neighbour just assumed that we had been to the dentist, and advised me not to talk or the cold might get in. Little did she realize she had just given me an excuse for not talking to anyone. On the way home Mum did some shopping. We must have met half the people we knew in Attercliffe, all wanting to stop for a chat. I was more than thankful to get home that day. I asked Mum to lock the door and if anyone came, to give me enough time to get upstairs. I didn't want anyone to see me this way, not even Mrs. Kerkhoff. When she did eventually knock on the door for her morning cup of tea with Mum, I was half way up the stairs. Mum suggested, in a louder than normal voice, "I've made the tea Kerkhoff but lets have it in your house this morning shall we? I sat on the stairs until the house went quiet. While I was on my own horror struck me. I was meeting Louise outside work that night and when my sister tells her that I am ill, Louise would call to see me instead. When Mum came back I explained to her about Louise. I couldn't go and speak. She wouldn't understand a word and I didn't want her to turn up and think that I was trying to dodge her, which is what I would have been doing, I suppose. Mum gave me a solution. "Why don't you write her a little note, telling her that you will get in touch as soon as you are able and I will tell her the truth. Louise is a very understanding person and discreet with it. If I tell her not to say anything to anyone you know she won't."

Mum came back from seeing Louise and said "She says that what you look like didn't matter to her, but I asked her to consider your feelings. She sends her love and she's got tickets for the show."

We got to the dentist for one o'clock the next day. My teeth were ready and waiting and the dentist said that an appointment for the hospital had been made for the following Monday. I went up to Louise's house. I saw her Mum and asked her to let Louise know that I would be seeing her on Saturday. On Monday morning the long trecks backwards and forwards to the hospital began again.

While I was on one of these journeys I reflected how many times Mum had done this over the years. It was a distance of sixteen miles round trip, on two forms of transport that would be very cold in winter and very hot in summer. I was beginning to realize what toils she would have had to endure and yet, she never complained once about the time and energy it had taken to get me this far. I hoped that I would never let her down if she ever needed me.

CHAPTER 7

MAKING PLANS AND CHANGING PLACES

The Cutlers hall drinks were always expensive, so we would go around to the Museum pub for the drinks. If it was a good night we would stay there instead of going back to the dance. We would return to the hall only to collect our shoes and coats. On one of these nights we got talking to two men who had been in the pub, more often than not, when we went in. They were doing a crossword puzzle but they hadn't got a pen, so Louise lent them hers. After this we became friends. When they came to sit at our table it was Brian who was interested in Louise and they started to pair off in the pub. That left Lewis, Barbara and myself. I soon started to feel like a gooseberry so at times I would make an excuse to go back to the dance with some of the other crowd and leave the four of them to get on with it. They included me in their company whenever they were planing an outing for the day and it worked out fine.

One day Louise came down to our house with the news that Lewis had stopped seeing Barbara. I was sympathetic towards them because I had been there myself, so I knew what they must be feeling like. The following week we went out as normal, meeting in the pub until the dance crowd got there, then I would go with them. This week it didn't work out like that. I arrived at the Museum and she was on her own. Fearing the worst I asked where Brian was. "They have gone to Alfred Golds to learn how to dance." she replied. Half the drink went down my throat, but on the outside. I almost choked. "Never, why?" I asked. "If I tell you, you won't let on will you?" she replied. "No" I said. I would have agreed to do anything then. I was so intrigued. "They are learning to dance because Lewis would like to go out with you." she said. "Forget it." I replied. "There is no chance. He and Barbara can patch it up."

I started to hatch a plan to get Barbara back into the life of Lewis Hunt. I would ask her to come out with me one night then, just by chance, we would find ourselves in the pub. We were sat in the pub when Brian and Louise came in. I thought Lewis hadn't come but he had taken a detour by way of the toilets. He came in a few minutes later and said "Hello" to us both. Barbara and I were sat at a table and I was hoping that the others would follow, but they didn't. They stayed at the bar. My little plan to get them sat together hadn't worked. They hardly spoke to each other at all, so 'B' and I left, leaving the three of them in the pub.

A few nights later Louise was pleading with me to come and meet Lewis on my own. She said "He really does want to go out with you. He says that if he had known before what he was letting himself in for, he would definitely have chosen you. Please Anne. Come if it's only to make up a foursome for tonight. I'm not asking you to go out with him on a permanent basis, just as friends. That's all." She was very persuasive, but there was no way I was going to walk into the pub on my own. It was up to her to call for me on that Saturday night. She said that she would be calling around seven o'clock. It was almost seven forty five and I had given her up. I laid on the settee, I had no make-up on, I hadn't combed my hair and I was reading a newspaper. I had resigned myself to a night in with no regrets. Then there was a sharp knock on the door. It flew open with Louise saying "I'm sorry I'm late, but I've been with Brian all afternoon. I've left him and Lewis in the pub" and, in the same breath, she said "Why aren't you ready?" I replied "I was going out at seven o'clock but somebody didn't get here until now. I told you I wasn't going to get ready until you got here."

She grabbed a comb and started to comb my hair while I put my make up on. I reached for my shoes as she got my coat. It was the quickest I had got ready and this for a first date. However, we had a good laugh at her expense when I saw how flushed she had gone. She had an allergy to cats and we had one. By the time she had got me out of the house her nose was streaming and her eyes were running and itching. In a friendly dig I just said "It serves you right."

As we arrived at the pub I got a feeling that I was going to see

Lewis for the first time in my life. The feeling was strange because I already knew him. So why was I feeling like this? As we went in I hung back so that she would be the first through the door. The two of them were sat in their usual place, behind the door on high stools, drinking and talking with the landlord of the establishment. Louise picked up half a glass of beer from the bar. She had obviously left it to come and get me. After taking a good drink she put it down saying "Anne, meet Lewis. I think you two have met haven't you?" Taken with a pinch of humour we both said "Yes." After that, it was a good night out, but the time I was dreading had arrived. After we had said good night to Louise and Brian, we walked to where I would catch my tram home. We had just missed one so there was at least fifteen minutes to wait for the next one. I thought it would have been easy to say "It's been a nice evening. I'll see you in the pub." However, I found myself giving him excuses why it wasn't a good idea to go out with me. I was saying "Nothing ever lasts so lets just keep friends, shall we?" But the response shouldn't have been a kiss on the lips, with a promise to meet on Tuesday in the pub. On the tram I couldn't believe that I had said yes.

It was the March 7th 1959 and I had just gone back on everything I had promised myself not to do. I wanted to change my mind. I wanted to ring him up and tell him that I valued him as a friend, and could we keep it that way. I didn't even know where he lived and I doubted very much that he would have a phone. So I resigned myself to the fact that I had to see him on Tuesday. I turned up late on purpose, so that if he wasn't in I could just ask the landlord, Mr. Drinkwater, if he had seen Louise in the pub that night. I didn't need any excuses. He was there and, I must admit, I was glad I had turned up. I could tell he was very pleased to see me.

It was not long after we had met that I began having problems with the roof of my mouth. It felt swollen and uncomfortable, so I had to get in touch with Fulwood Hospital. They told me to go to the Sheffield Royal Hospital where I would see Mr. Hynes. Mr. Hynes looked visibly older now, however, his manner was still as impeccable as ever. He looked in my mouth and, with a puzzled look, he said "We've got a lump growing Annie. Now you know what I'm going to say don't you? It will have to come out. It's not serious, at least not yet, so the sooner we have you in the better. All right? We'll send for you in the next few days. Good-bye, take care now." That was the last time I remember seeing Mr. Hynes.

I had told Lewis about some of the times in hospital and about some of the operations that I had had done, but I still don't think he knew how to take it, that I had to go in for yet another one. I was dreading the thought that I wouldn't be able to wear my dentures after the operation and there was no way I was going to let Lewis see me without my top teeth. The thought scared me so much that I asked him to telephone the hospital first before he came to visit. If I couldn't wear teeth I was not going to have visitors, not even my Mother.

The day before I was due to go into the hospital, Lewis came to take me out. He had brought with him a big parcel. He said that it was a belated twenty first birthday present. I took the gift wrapping off to reveal a large square box. I opened it and turned back the tissue paper to see the most luxurious, pale rose pink colour. As it lay in the box I could see a cape collar, with nylon embroidered lace around the edge. As I took it out of the box I held it by the shoulders so that it uncurled to reveal a full length, nylon and silk dressing gown. It was finely padded all the way through. It was sewn in a crisscross pattern so that the sewing formed inch squares through the whole garment. It was far too glamorous for the hospital, but I was twenty-one and in love.

The lump was removed with very little discomfort and I was able to put my teeth back in almost at once, which was a good thing because Lewis never rang. He just came up and straight into the ward. For the three days that I was in hospital everyone admired my fabulous dressing gown. It was almost worth going into hospital for.

We began to go out more and more on our own, rather than in a foursome. However, whenever we did go out with Brian and Louise we enjoyed the camaraderie and friendship. Louise and Brian were married on March 26th 1960 and Lewis was asked to be the best man. Lewis and I decided to get engaged on September 15th 1960, Lewis's birthday. We named the day and told our parents to look forward to a wedding within the next year. We began to save, but the job I was doing wasn't well paid, so I started a job at The Tempered Spring Co. It was target work. It was hard and, at first, I got tiny splinters in my fingers from the wire we had to use to make the little springs from. I made the little springs that went into typewriters. It was monotonous work and I was always tired from the long hours and overtime I was

Lewis and myself, 1959. I was wearing one of the dresses I had made

My Grandmother and her husband, Uncle Bill at Skegness

Lewis Hunt in Castleton, 1960

putting in. However, I had something to work for; we were buying a house. Gran had offered to let us stay at her house if we hadn't enough saved for the house and the wedding. So there was no great panic to get the house, but I wanted the perfect wedding.

It was in 1960 that we took our last ride on the trams. Sheffield had made it's mind up to get rid of them because they caused all sorts of problems for other road users. The tracks used to run up the centre of the road and when passengers waiting at the stops saw one coming they would step out into the road with little regard for the oncoming traffic. So some of the accidents were blamed on the trams, irrespective of who's fault it really was. The last tram journey was October 8th 1960. It was a cold wet night and there was a very nostalgic feeling among the crowds. They had gathered to wave good-bye to the end of an era. As the tram passed by, people were putting coins on the lines so that the tram would bend it. It was like the last foot print of an old friend.

When the first snowfall came that winter every one was mourning the passing of the trams. The buses got stuck on the icy and muddy roads. Some outer districts didn't see any public transport for days until the roads had been cleared.

I was the cause of a fight between two men when Lewis and I travelled to Rotherham on the bus. We decided to have a night out in Rotherham. The bus was full, but we had separate seats on the upper deck. He was sat at the back and I was sat next to a chap. We got talking about nothing special. The weather would have come into it as usual, then we began to sense a conversation going on behind us. It was a couple of young men and one of them was using me as the subject of their offensive and insulting conversation. It was obvious that he thought I was on my own. The chap at the side of me could see that I was getting annoyed about it. He was looking at me and said "It's not worth it love." He laid a hand on my arm and gave it a little squeeze. The bus pulled into the stop. It was a terminus so everyone had to get off. I got out of my seat just as the speaker was getting up. As he looked up at me I said, in a very calm and unnatural voice, "Thank God you're not like me and I will thank God I'm not like you." I felt two hands on my shoulders. The man behind was holding me as if to let the offender know that I had got some support. Then my companion pushed passed me to walk behind the trouble maker. Lewis was oblivious to everything that had gone off. As we got off the bus my companion was knocking seven bells out of the mouth man and he was winning. I wished I could have thanked my 'knight', but I think it was better this way. I told Lewis what had happened over a drink and well into the night.

Our wedding day was eight weeks away. We had asked Lewis's sister, Pat, to be a bridesmaid and one of his nieces. The other two would be my sisters, Joyce and Ivy. I had started to think about the wedding dress and the brides maid's dresses. I had always known that I would make my own wedding dress. I asked Mum if she would like to go with me to get the materials for it. She was more than pleased that I had asked her. So on the following Saturday morning I got up early and made a cup of tea for myself and Mum. She was still in bed so I took hers up to her. She asked "Have you got your money out of the bank love?" I nodded. I still couldn't believe I was going to buy the fabric for my wedding dress. As soon as Mum came downstairs she got ready to go out and I asked "Aren't you going to have any breakfast?" She shook her head saying "I'll have some when I get back." We had never been shopping so early on a Saturday morning. It was just turned nine o'clock when we walked into Banners stores. In those days it was a big departmental store, ranging from the cheaper goods to the better class goods and it gave one a certain feeling of satisfaction when you could pay with cash, instead of the Banners cheques, for such a large order. I bought ten yards of ivory brocade. It cost six pounds a yard, a small fortune then. I was going to make the two small dresses of the four bridesmaids I was having. So, I bought a pink fabric with a delicate little flower on it. It was almost like a chiffon. We went round to see Gran and Mum took sheer delight in showing the material to her. I made her promise not to show it to all and sundry and she agreed. "But can I just show it to Kerkhoff?" Mum pleaded. I would have loved to do it myself but I gave her the pleasure instead.

I was surprised and happy at how the whole dress was coming together, with very few problems. I had several more problems with the bridesmaid dresses though. I had to wait for them to come for fittings and the lace trimmings had to be put on by hand, but I got them done with plenty of time to spare. It's a pity that the groom misses all this side of getting married. I was thoroughly enjoying myself until my grandmother dropped a bombshell six weeks before the wedding. We

Waiting to get married 1961

Just a few weeks to go now

My father in typical pose at the club

had gone to see her. She was not her usual self. I asked her what was wrong. "Have you got your house sorted out yet?" she asked. "No" I replied. "Oh. I was hopping you had." "Why?" I asked. "Because me and Uncle Bill have been thinking that it would be better if you could start your married life in a place of your own, instead of here." I heard quite clearly what she was telling us. When I said "But it's only six weeks to the wedding Gran" the silence spread through the house and it was not going to go away. We said our good-byes and I promised to see her the following week. Lewis and I didn't speak. We seemed to just go into our own trains of thought. It lasted until we met Mum and Dad in the club. While Lewis was at the bar and Dad was playing snooker I said to Mum "Do you know what Gran has told us?" Her answer didn't come as a surprise to me. "Yes love. She wanted me to tell you, but I couldn't and besides, it's your business not mine. I said "I don't know what to do Mum." "You'll cope somehow. Don't worry" she replied.

A week went by and Lewis and I were looking around for accommodation, but there was none. I got talking to a girl where I worked and she said that her father was selling their house. I told her that we hadn't got a lot of money left to buy a house with, but she insisted that it wouldn't hurt to have a word with her father. So we agreed to go to see the house. It was at the top of a big hill. It was small and it was the end of a terrace. Looking at it I didn't much like it, but the deal we had been offered was not to be scoffed at. Her father had offered to waive the deposit, and he offered to pay the solicitors' fee if we had the same solicitors as theirs. The only thing we would have to pay for was the stamp duty and search fees. We left the house as the prospective owners. We had got our house.

On the day we were given the keys we had only three weeks to get the house fit to live in after our honeymoon. It was hard work, but it was ours. Every spare minute we had we put into the house. We were thankful that they had left the curtains up. When we took the old lino up in the front room we found that the floor boards were rotten and would need to be replaced. So we had that done instead of redecorating the bedrooms. We decided to make two rooms comfortable to live in; They would be the front bedroom and the tiny middle room that doubled as a dining room. The day before the wedding day we were laying the linoleum, ready for the carpet. At around four o'clock that day we closed the door on 61 Mount Road, Parkwood Springs. The next time we were to walk in would be as Mr. and Mrs.

At three o'clock on the morning of my wedding day I was wishing that I hadn't gone out with Mum and Dad and my brothers the night before. I had tipped the barrel once too often and now I was paying for it dearly. I was feeling sick, walking around the yard in my nightclothes, declaring "I'm not going to get married. I don't know why I ever agreed to do it." Apparently, I asked Mum if she thought I was in love. I eventually got back to bed where sleep came in shallow patterns. I was awoke by the sound of the postman knocking on the door. My brother got up to answer it then got back into bed. I got up and I felt awful. Downstairs I made myself a drink of tea, opened the wedding cards that had been delivered so noisily and then I just sat. So this was my wedding day.

Mum was the first one up. We had our breakfast together then slowly the whole house was filling up with people. Mum fetched Kerkhoff in to have a cup of tea with us before we went shopping. I had to get some stiffening for the big bridesmaids dresses to give them a little more body. When we got back it was ten o'clock. Mum and I set to and made the two skirts that would go under the bridesmaids dresses. We started the countdown to the wedding. I had three hours to go. As we were eating our fish and chip dinner from the chip shop, Lewis's sister and niece arrived. They were the other half of the bridesmaids. It was then that it hit me. From this day my life was going to be different. Mum was saying "Are you all right love?" I just nodded my head. To speak would have been too much. I just wanted to be by myself, just for a few minutes. But where was there in a house buzzing with people all looking too happy? I disappeared to the toilet across the yard. After a while someone tapped on the door. It was Mum. "Are you all right Anne?" she asked. I opened the door and she could see that I had been crying. She put her arm around me and said "I know it's hard, but you will be happy Nanc. I know you will." I went back to the house to start getting dressed. I had one hour to make myself into a bride for Lewis.

As I went upstairs my two little bridesmaids were at the top. They looked lovely. I gave them a kiss and told them how beautiful they were. My sister Ivy followed me into the back bedroom. After I had put my make up on she and my mother helped me to get dressed. Mum fastened my veil to my hair and then put the tiara on. I had long hair, but I had taken it up into two French rolls. One was rolled length ways down the back of my head and the other was across the middle. Mum filtered the tiara around this one. My dressing was complete. My sister had gone downstairs to wait for the cars that would take the bridesmaids to church. As the cars arrived I was helped down the stairs by my Mum and Dad. It was the first time I had seen tears in a man's eyes. At the bottom of the stairs Mum kissed me then turned quickly away to get into one of the cars with the bridesmaids. The silver sixpence she had pressed into my hand I put into the little handkerchief pocket in the side of my dress.

The quiet of the house was unreal. I didn't know what to say to my father, while we waited for the car to come back for us. I looked around the room. The black lead fire place looked brighter, even without a fire. I just wished there could have been a fire lit in the grate but it was too warm. The new sideboard still looked a bit odd there. I thought about the many hours I had spent trying to make the old one shine a little brighter. The pegged rug had been taken up. Due to it's bulkiness Mum was afraid that someone might trip over it, so it had been rolled up and put at the back of the settee. I could just see a corner of it. A lot of happy hours were spent making that rug. I didn't see the car arrive. Dad put his arm around me and said "I'll miss thee lass." then he kissed me. "Pull my veil over Dad." I asked and as he did I allowed a tear to roll down my face. "Lets go" he said as he linked my arm in his.

We arrived at Attercliffe Church just as the clock was striking three. On the way here I was hoping that the rain would stop, and it did. I had to hold my dress up, off the rain soaked pavement and manoeuvre around the puddles on the church drive. At the church door I let it fall to the floor. My bridesmaids made sure that the hem was down and that the train at the back was straight. My veil was short to the waist allowing the big bow at the back of the dress to be seen. I turned to Dad who was holding my bouquet and as he handed me the flowers he winked. I was ready to get married. The church was full and I was surprised to see people standing at the back. I recognized friends, neighbours and workmates from three of the places I had worked at. I could hear the organ playing our special request 'I'll Walk Beside You.' As I started to walk down the isle it changed to the traditional tune "Here Comes The Bride."

It was August 19th 1961. Here we were in front of the alter, centre stage with the rest of our lives waiting in the wings. A life that was to yield four perfect sons and more happiness than I had a right to hope for. As we turned to take our first steps as Mr. and Mrs. Hunt, the organ began to play again 'I'll Walk Beside You'.

****

Our wedding day, 1961.
From the baby girl, some suggested should be let to die, came the happiest married woman. From one who was told she couldn't sew to one who even made her own wedding dress.

'Mr. & Mrs. Hunt' on their honeymoon

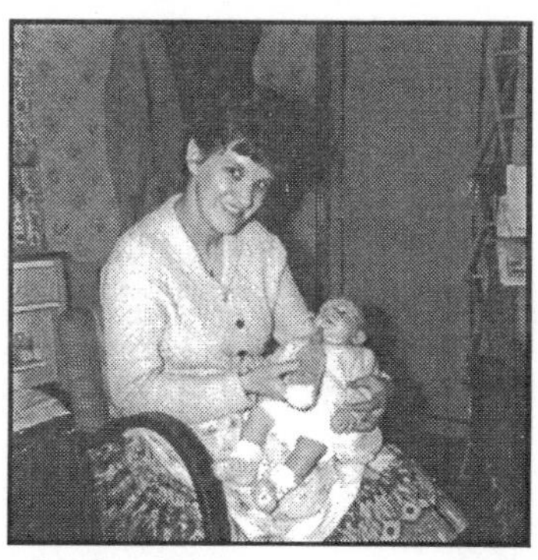

Our first baby, Anthony, born 1962